Creati
FATE

James Allen (1864–1912) retired from the business world to pursue a lifestyle of writing and contemplation. His books are classics in the fields of inspiration and spirituality. Although *As a Man Thinketh* is his most popular work, he authored several other books that deal with the power of thought, including *The Path of Prosperity*, *Eight Pillars of Prosperity* and *James Allen's Book of Meditations for Every Day in the Year*.

Creating Your FATE

The Power of Shaping Your Life's Story

JAMES ALLEN

RUPA

Published by
Rupa Publications India Pvt. Ltd 2024
7/16, Ansari Road, Daryaganj
New Delhi 110002

P-ISBN: 978-93-5702-654-3
E-ISBN: 978-93-5702-659-8

Fourth impression 2024

10 9 8 7 6 5 4

CONTENTS

1

ENERGY AND POWER

How wonderful is the universal energy! Never-tiring, inexhaustible, and apparently eternal in its operation, it moves in atom and in star, informing the fleeting shapes of tune with its restless, glowing, pulsating power.

Man is a portion of this creative energy, and in him it manifests, through a combination of mental faculties, as affection, passion, intelligence, morality, reason, understanding, and wisdom. He is not merely a blind conductor of energy, but he consciously uses, controls, and directs it. Slowly, but with certainty, is he gaining control of the forces without, and is making them do obedient service. And just as surely will he gain control of the forces within—the subtle energies of thought—and direct them into channels of harmony and happiness.

Man's true place in the Cosmos is that of a king, not a slave, a commander under the law of Good and not a helpless tool in the reign of Evil. His own body and mind are the dual dominion over which he is to reign, a Lord of Truth, the master of himself, the wise user and controller of his store of pure, eternal, creative energy. Let him walk the earth unashamed, strong, valiant, tender, and kind; no longer prostrate in self-abasement, but walking erect in the dignity of perfect manhood; not groveling in selfishness and remorse, nor crying for pardon and mercy, but standing firm and free in the sublime majesty of a sinless life.

Long has man regarded himself as vile, weak, and unworthy, and has been content to remain so. But in the new era which has just now burst upon the world, he is to make a glorious discovery that he is pure, powerful, and noble when he rises up and wills. The rising up is not against any outward enemy; not against neighbor, nor governments, nor laws, nor spirits, nor principalities, but against the ignorance, folly, and misery which beset him in the dominion of his own mind. For it is only by ignorance and folly that man is slavish; by knowledge and wisdom his kingdom is restored.

Let them who will, preach man's weakness and helplessness, but I will teach his strength and power. I write for men, not for babes; for those who are eager to learn, and earnest to achieve; for those who will put away (for the world's good) a petty personal indulgence, a selfish desire, a mean thought, and live on as though it were not, without craving and regret. The Truth is not for the frivolous and the thoughtless. The Life Triumphant is not for triflers and loiterers.

Man is a master. If he were not, he could not act contrary to law. Thus his so-called weakness is an indication of strength; his sin is the inversion of his capacity for holiness. For what is his weakness and sin but misdirected energy, misapplied power? In this sense, the wrongdoer is strong, not weak; but he is ignorant, and exerts his strength in wrong directions instead of right, against the law of things instead of with it.

Suffering is the recoil of misdirected strength, The bad man becomes good by reversing his conduct. If you are weeping over your sins, cease to commit those sins and establish yourself in their opposing virtues. It is thus that weakness is converted into strength, helplessness into power, and suffering into bliss. By turning his energies from the old channels of vice, and directing them into the new channels of virtue, the sinner becomes a saint.

USE AND MISUSE OF ENERGY

While the universal energy may be unlimited, in particular forms its sum is strictly limited. A man is possessed of a given amount of energy, and he can use it or misuse it, can conserve and concentrate it, or dissipate and disperse it. Power is concentrated energy; wisdom is that energy adapted to beneficent ends. He is the man of influence and power who directs all his energies towards one great purpose, and patiently works and waits for its fulfillment, sacrificing his desires in other and more pleasant directions. He is the man of folly and weakness who, thinking chiefly of pleasure, gratifies the desire of the hour, or follows the whim and impulse of the moment, and so drifts thoughtlessly into peevishness and poverty of mind.

The energy used in one direction is not available for use in other directions; this is a universal law both in mind and matter. Emerson calls it "the law of compensation." Gain in a given direction necessitates loss in its opposite direction. The force placed in one scale is deducted from the other scale. Nature is always endeavoring to strike a balance. The energy which is dissipated in idleness is not given to work. The pleasure-seeker cannot also be a Truth-seeker.

The force wasted in a fit of bad temper is drawn from the man's store of virtue, particularly the virtue of patience. Spiritually, this law of compensation is the law of sacrifice. Selfish pleasure must be sacrificed if purity is to be gained; hatred must be yielded up if love is to be acquired; vice must be renounced if virtue is to be embraced.

Earnest men soon discover that if they are to accomplish anything that is successful, strong, and enduring, in worldly, intellectual, or spiritual channels, they must curb their desires, and sacrifice much that seems sweet; yea, even much that seems important.

Hobbies, bodily and mental indulgences, enticing companionships, alluring pleasures, and all work that does not tend to some central purpose in his life must be sacrificed by the man of strong resolve. He opens his eyes to the fact that time and energy are strictly limited, and so he economizes the one and concentrates the other.

Foolish men waste their energies in swinish ease and gluttonous indulgence, in frivolous pleasures and empty talk, in hateful thoughts and irritable outbursts of passion, in vain controversy and meddlesome interference. They then complain that many are more "fortunately equipped than they are for a useful, successful, or great life, and they envy their honored neighbor who has sacrificed self to duty, and has devoted all his energies to the faithful performance of the business of his life.

"He who is just, speaks the truth, and does what is his own business, him the world will hold dear." Let a man attend to his own business, concentrating all his energies upon the perfect accomplishment of the task of his life, not stepping aside to condemn or interfere with the duties of others, and he will find life simple, strong, and happy.

THE TRUTH OF LIFE

The universe is girt with goodness and strength, and it protects the strong and the good. Evil and weakness are self-destructive. Dissipation is annihilation. All nature loves strength. I see no inherent cruelty in "the survival of the fittest." It is a spiritual as well as a natural law. The stronger qualities of the beast are the fittest to evolve a higher type. The nobler moral qualities in man are his emancipators, and it is well that they should dominate and ultimately crush out the ignoble tendencies.

Most certain it is that he who gives dominion to the lower,

courts destruction, and does not survive, either in the struggle of life without or the battle of Truth within. The life given to the lower is lost to the higher; yea, it is finally lost also to the lower, and so all is lost, for evil is ultimately nothingness. But the life given to the higher is preserved, and is not lost to anything, for, while it sacrifices much that the world holds precious, it does not sacrifice anything that is precious in reality.

The untrue and worthless must perish, and he who consecrates himself to the good and the true is content that they should perish, and so at last he stands where sacrifice ends, and all is gain—such a one survives in the struggle of life without, and he conquers in the battle of Truth within.

First, then, be strong. Strength is the firm basis on which is built the temple of the Triumphant Life.

Without a central motive and fixed resolve, your life will be a poor, weak, drifting, unstable thing. Let the act of the moment be governed by the deep abiding purpose of the heart. You will act differently at different times, but the act will not be wrong if the heart is right. You may fall and go astray at times, especially under great stress, but you will quickly regain yourself, and you will grow wiser and stronger, thereby, so long as you guide yourself by the moral compass within, and do not throw it away to gratify indulgence and give yourself up to uncertain drifting.

Follow your conscience. Be true to your convictions. Do at the moment what you regard as right, and put away all procrastination, vacillation, and fear. If you are convinced that in the performance of your duty under certain circumstances the severest measures are necessary, carry out those measures, and let there be no uncertainty about it. Err on the side of strength rather than weakness. The measures you adopt may not be the best, but if they are the best you know, then your plain duty is to carry them out. By so doing you will discover the better way, if you are anxious for progress, and are willing to learn. Deliberate beforehand, but in the tune of action do not hesitate.

Avoid anger and stubbornness, lust and greed. The angry man is the weak man. The stubborn man, who refuses to learn or mend his ways, is the foolish man. He grows old in folly, and grey hairs do not bring him reverence or honor. The sensualist has energy for pleasure only, and reserves none for manliness and self-respect. The greedy man is blind to the nobility of human nature and the glory of a true life; he spends his energies in perpetuating the miseries of hell, instead of enjoying the happiness of heaven.

Your strength is with you, and you can spend it in burrowing downward or in climbing upward. You can dissipate it in selfishness or conserve it in goodness. The same energy will enable you to become a beast or a god. The course along which you direct it will determine its effect. Do not think the thought, "My mind is weak," but convert weakness into strength, and energy into power by redirecting your mental forces. Turn your thoughts into noble channels. Put away vain longings and foolish regrets; abolish complaint and self-condolence, and have no dalliance with evil. Lift your face upward. Rise up in your divine strength, and spurn from your mind and life all meanness and weakness. Do not live the false life of a whining slave, but live the true life of a conquering master.

2

RIGHT BEGINNINGS

"All common things, each day's events,
That with the hour begin and end;
Our pleasures and our discontents
Are rounds by which we may ascend."

"We have not wings, we cannot soar;
But we have feet to scale and climb."

—Longfellow

"For common life, its wants
And ways, would I set forth in beauteous hues."

—Browning

Life is full of beginnings. They are presented every day and every hour to every person. Most beginnings are small, and appear trivial and insignificant, but in reality they are the most important things in life.

See how in the material world everything proceeds from small beginnings. The mightiest river is at first a rivulet over which the grasshopper could leap; the great flood commences with a few drops of rain; the sturdy oak, which has endured the storms of a thousand winters, was once an acorn; and the smouldering match, carelessly dropped, may be the means of devastating a whole town by fire.

Consider, also, how in the spiritual world the greatest things proceed from smallest beginnings. A light fancy may be the inception of a wonderful invention or an immortal work of art; a spoken sentence may turn the tide of history; a pure thought entertained may lead to the exercise of a world-wide regenerative power; and a momentary animal impulse may lead to the darkest crime.

Have you yet discovered the vast importance of beginnings? Do you really know what is involved in a beginning? Do you know the number of beginnings you are continously making, and realise their full import? If not, come with me for a short time, and thoughtfully explore this much ignored byway of blessedness, for blessed it is when wisely resorted to, and much strength and comfort it holds for the understanding mind.

A BEGINNING IS IN ITSELF AN END

A beginning is a cause, and as such it must be followed by an effect, or a train of effects, and the effect will always be of the same nature as the cause. The nature of an initial impulse will always determine the body of its results. A beginning also presupposes an ending, a consummation, achievement, or goal. A gate leads to a path, and the path leads to some particular destination; so a beginning leads to results, and results lead to a completion.

There are right beginnings and wrong beginnings, which are followed by effects of a like nature. You can, by careful thought, avoid wrong beginnings and make right beginnings, and so escape evil results and enjoy good results.

There are beginnings over which you have no control and authority- these are without, in the universe, in the world of nature around you, and in other people who have the same liberty as yourself.

Do not concern yourself with these beginnings, but direct your energies and attention to those beginnings over which you have complete control and authority, and which bring about the complicated web of results which compose your life. These beginnings are to be found in the realm of your own thoughts and actions; in your mental attitude under the variety of circumstances through which you pass; in your conduct day by day—in short, in your life as you make it, which is your world of good or ill.

In aiming at the life of Blessedness one of the simplest beginnings to be considered and rightly made is that which we all make everyday—namely, the beginning of each day's life.

How do you begin each day? At what hour do you rise? How do you commence your duties? In what frame of mind do you enter upon the sacred life of a new day? What answer can you give your heart to these important questions? You will find that much happiness or unhappiness follows upon the right or wrong beginning of the day, and that, when every day is wisely begun, happy and harmonious sequences will mark its course, and life in its totality will not fall far short of the ideal blessedness.

It is a right and strong beginning to the day to rise at an early hour. Even if your worldly duty does not demand it, it is wise to make of it a duty, and begin the day strongly by shaking off indolence. How are you to develop strength of will and mind and body if you begin every day by yielding to weakness? Self-indulgence is always followed by unhappiness. People who lie in bed till a late hour are never bright and cheerful and fresh, but are the prey of irritabilities, depressions, debilities, nervous disorders, abnormal fancies, and all unhappy moods. This is the heavy price which they have to pay for their daily indulgence. Yet, so blinding is the pandering to self that, like the drunkard who takes his daily dram in the belief that it is bracing up the nerves which it is all the time shattering, so the lie-a-bed is convinced that long hours of ease are necessary for him as a possible remedy for those very moods and weaknesses and disorders of which his indulgence is the cause. Men and women are totally unaware of the great losses which they entail by this common indulgence: loss of strength both of mind and body, loss of prosperity, loss of knowledge, and loss of happiness.

Begin the day, then, by rising early. If you have no object in doing so, never mind; get up, and go out for a gentle walk among the beauties of nature, and you will experience a buoyancy, a freshness, and a delight, not to say a peace of mind, which will amply reward you for your effort. One good effort is followed by another; and when a man begins the day by rising early, even though with no other purpose in view, he will find that the silent early hour is conducive to clearness of mind and calmness of thought, and that his early morning walk is enabling him to become a consecutive thinker, and so to see life and its problems, as well as himself and his affairs, in a clearer light; and so in time he will rise early with the express purpose of preparing and harmonising his mind to meet any and every difficulty with wisdom and calm strength.

There is, indeed, a spiritual influence in the early morning hour, a divine silence and an inexpressible repose, and he who, purposeful and strong, throws off the mantle of ease and climbs the hills to greet the morning sun will thereby climb no inconsiderable distance up the hills of blessedness and truth.

The right beginning of the day will be followed by cheerfulness at the morning meal, permeating the house-hold with a sunny influence; and the tasks and duties of the day will be undertaken in a strong and confident spirit, and the whole day will be well lived.

Then there is a sense in which every day may be regarded as the beginning of a new life, in which one can think, act, and live newly, and in a wiser and better spirit.

"Every day is a fresh beginning;
Every morn is the world made new,
Ye who are weary of sorrow and sinning,
Here is a beautiful hope for you,
A hope for me and a hope for you."

THOUGHTS AS BUILDING BLOCKS

Do not dwell upon the sins and mistakes of yesterday so exclusively as to have no energy and mind left for living rightly today, and do not think that the sins of yesterday can prevent you from living purely today. Begin today aright, and, aided by the accumulated experiences of all your past days, live it better than any of your previous days; but you cannot possibly live it better unless you begin it better. The character of the whole day depends upon the way it is begun.

Another beginning which is of great importance is the beginning of any particular and responsible undertaking. How does a man begin the building of a house? He first secures a plan of the proposed edifice and then proceeds to build according to the plan, scrupulously following it in every detail, beginning with the foundation. Should he neglect the beginning—namely, the obtaining of a mathematical plan—his labour would be wasted, and his building, should it reach completion without tumbling to pieces, would be insecure and worthless. The same law holds good in any important work: the right beginning and first essential is a definite mental plan on which to build. Nature will have no slipshod work, no slovenliness, and she annihilates confusion, or rather, confusion is in itself annihilation. Order, definiteness, purpose eternally and universally prevail, and he who in his operations ignores these mathematical elements at once deprives himself of substantiality, completeness, success.

"Life without a plan,
As useless as the moment it began,
Serves merely as a soil for discontent
To thrive in, an encumbrance ere half spent."

Let a man start in business without having in his mind a perfectly formed plan to systematically pursue and he will be incoherent in his efforts and will fail in his business operations. The laws which must be observed in the building of a house also operate in the building up of a business. A definite plan is followed by coherent effort; and coherent effort is followed by well-knit and orderly results—to wit, completeness, perfection, success, happiness.

But not only mechanical and commercial enterprise—all undertakings, of whatsoever nature, come under this law. The author's book, the artist's picture, the orator's speech, the reformer's work, the inventor's machine, the general's campaign, are all carefully planned in the mind before the attempt to actualise them is commenced; and in accordance with the unity, solidarity, and perfection of the original mental plan will be the actual and ultimate success of the undertaking.

Successful men, influential men, good men are those who, amongst other things, have learned the value and utilised the power which lies hidden in those obscure beginnings which the foolish man passes by as "insignificant."

But the most important beginning of all—that upon which afflication or blessedness inevitably depends, yet is most neglected and least understood—is the inception of thought in the hidden, but causal region of the mind. Your whole life is a series of effects having their cause in thought—in your own thought. All conduct is made and moulded by thought; all deeds, good or bad, are thoughts made visible. A seed put into the ground is the beginning of a plant or tree; the seed germinates, the plant or tree comes forth into the light and evolves. A thought put into the mind is the beginning of a line of conduct: the thought first sends down its roots into the mind, and then pushes forth into the light in the forms of actions or conduct, which evolve into character and destiny.

Hateful, angry, envious, covetous, and impure thoughts are wrong beginnings, which lead to painful results. Loving, gentle, kind, unselfish and pure thoughts are right beginnings, which lead to blissful results. This is so simple, so plain, so absolutely true! and yet how neglected, how evaded, and how little understood!

The gardener who most carefully studies how, when, and where to put in his seeds obtains the best results and gains the greater horticultural knowledge. The best crops gladden the soul of him who makes the best beginning. The man who most patiently studies how to put into his mind the seeds of strong, wholesome, and charitable thoughts, will obtain the best results in life, and will gain greater knowledge of truth. The greatest blessedness comes to him, who infuses into his mind the purest and noblest thoughts.

None but right acts can follow right thoughts; none but a right life can follow right acts—and by living a right life all blessedness is achieved.

He who considers the nature and import of his thoughts, who strives daily to eliminate bad thoughts and supplant them with good, comes at last to see that thoughts are the beginnings of results which affect every fibre of his being, which potently influence every event and circumstance of his life. And when he thus sees, he thinks only right thoughts, chooses to make only those mental beginnings which lead to peace and blessedness.

Wrong thoughts are painful in their inception, painful in their growth, and painful in their fruitage. Right thoughts are blissful in their inception, blissful in their growth, and blissful in their fruitage.

Many are the right beginnings which a man must discover and

adopt on his way to wisdom; but that which is first and last, most important and all embracing, which is the source and fountain of all abiding happiness, is the right beginning of the mental operations—this implies the steady development of self-control, will-power, steadfastness, strength, purity, gentleness, insight, and comprehension. It leads to the perfecting of life, for he who thinks perfectly has abolished all unhappiness, his every moment is peaceful, his years are rounded with bliss—he has attained to the complete and perfect blessedness.

3

WORDS AND WISDOM

I would find
Where Wisdom is, where Peace abides, where Truth,
Majestic, changeless, and eternal, stands
Untouched by the illusions of the world;
For surely there is Knowledge, Truth, and Peace
For him who seeks.

Thoughts, words, acts—these combine to make up the entire life of every individual. Words and acts are thoughts expressed. We think in words. In the process of thinking, words are stored up in the consciousness, where they await expression and use as occasion may call them forth.

Words fit the mind which received them; they are the tally of the intellect which uses them. The meaner the mind, the more meagre is the vocabulary. A limited and a capacious intellect alike expresses itself through a limited and an extensive use of words. A great mind expresses itself by the vehicle of flowing and noble language.

Words stand for conceptions. Conceptions are embodied in words. At the moment that a conception is formed in the mind, its corresponding word arises in the thought. Conceptions and words cannot be hidden away indefinitely. Sooner or later they will come forth into the outer world of expression. The matter of the universe is in ceaseless circulation. Its hidden things are continuously coming forth into open and visible life. Likewise the mental operations of men are ever in active circulation, and their hidden thoughts are daily expressing themselves in words and acts. The words and actions of every man are determined by the thoughts in which he habitually dwells.

A WISE MAN ONCE SAID...

Speech is audible thought. A man reveals him. self through his speech. Whether he is pure or impure, foolish or vice, he makes his inner condition known through his speech. The foolish man is known by the way in which he talks ; the wise man is known by the purity, gravity, and excellence of his speech. "He who would gain a knowledge of men." says Confucius, "must first learn to understand the meaning of words "

All wise men, saints, and great teachers have declared that the first step in wisdom is to control the tongue. The disciple of speech is a mental disciple. When a man controls his tongue, he controls his mind; when he purifies his speech, he purifies his mind. Speech and mind cannot be separated. They are two aspects of character.

A man may read Scripture, study religions, and practise mystical arts; but if he allows his tongue to run loosely, he will be as foolish at the end of all his labours as he was at the beginning.

A man may not read Scripture, nor study religions, nor practise ascetic arts; but if he controls his tongue, and studies how to speak wisely and well, he will become wise.

Wisdom is perceived in the words which are its expression. We speak of certain men—of Shakespeare for instance—as being wise. We never saw Shakespeare, and we know very little of his life; how, then, do we know he was wise ? By his words only. Where there are wise words, we know there is a wise mind. A foolish man may, like a parrot, repeat wise words, but a wise man frames wise sentences ; his wisdom is shown in originally expressed language.

Why do men speak of words as being bad or good, degrading or inspiring, low or lofty, weak or strong? Is it not because they, unconsciously recognise that words cannot be dissociated from thoughts ? Why do pure-minded people avoid a man who habitually uses impure language ? Is is not because they know that such words proceed from an unclean mind ?

It is impossible for any being to give utterance to words which are not already lodged in his mind fit the form of thought. The impure mind cannot speak pure words; the pure mind cannot speak impure words. The ignorant cannot speak learnedly, nor the learned ignorantly. The foolish man cannot speak wisely, nor the wise foolishly.

Altered speech follows an altered mind. When a man turns from evil to good, his conversation becomes cleansed. As a man increases in wisdom, he watches, modifies, and perfects his speech.

If the foolish and the wise are known by their words, what, then, is the speech of folly, and what the language of wisdom? A man is foolish:

If he talks aimlessly and incoherently.
If he engages in impure conversations.
If he utters falsehood.
If he speaks ill of the absent, and carries
about evil reports concerning others.
If he frames flattering words.
If he utters violent and abusive words.

If his speech is irreverent, and
his words are directed against the great and good.
If he speaks in praise of himself.

A man is wise:

If he talks with purpose and intelligence.
If his conversation is chaste.
If he utters words of sincerity and truth.
If he speaks well of and in defence of, the absent.
If he speaks words of virtuous reproof.
If his speech is gentle and kindly.
If he talks reverently of the great and good.
If he speaks in praise of others.

We are all, now and always, justified and condemned by our words. The law of Truth is not held in abeyance, and every day is judgement day. For "every idle word" which one speaks he is at once "called to account" in an immediate and certain loss of happiness and influence. By the words which we habitually utter we publish to the universe the degree of our intelligence and the standard of our morality, and receive back through them the judgement of the world. The fool thinks he is harshly judged and badly treated by others, not knowing that his real scourge is his own ungoverned tongue.

To control the tongue, to discipline the speech, to strive for the use of purer and gentler words—this is a very lowly thing, and one that is much despised; but it cannot be neglected by him who eagerly aspires to walk the way of wisdom.

4

THE NATURE AND POWER OF MIND

Mind is the arbiter of life. It is the creator and shaper of conditions, and the recipient of its own results. It contains within itself both the power to create illusion and to perceive reality. Mind is the infallible weaver of destiny. Thought is the thread, good and evil deeds are the "warp and woof" or foundation, and the web, woven upon the loom of life, is character. Mind clothes itself in garments of its own making.

Man, as a mental being, possesses all the powers of mind, and is furnished with unlimited choice. He learns by experience, and he can accelerate or retard his experience. He is not arbitrarily bound at any point, but he has bound himself at many points, and having bound himself he can, when he chooses, liberate himself.

He can become bestial or pure, ignorant or noble, foolish or wise, just as he chooses. He can, by reoccurring practice, form habits, and he can, by renewed effort, break them off. He can surround himself with illusions until Truth is completely lost, and he can destroy each of those illusions until Truth is entirely recovered. His possibilities are endless; his freedom is complete.

THE ENLIGHTENED MIND

It is the nature of the mind to create its own conditions, and to choose the states in which it shall dwell. It also has the power to alter any condition, to abandon any state. This it is continually doing as it gathers knowledge of state after state by repeated choice and exhaustive experience.

Inward processes of thought make up the sum of character and life. Man can modify and alter these processes by bringing will and effort to bear upon them. The bonds of habit, impotence, and sin are self-made, and can only be destroyed by one's self. They exist nowhere but in one's mind, and although they are directly related to outward things, they have no real existence in those things.

The outer is molded and animated by the inner, and never the inner by the outer. Temptation does not arise in the outer object, but in the lust of the mind for that object. Nor do sorrow and suffering belong by nature to the external things and happenings of life, but in an undisciplined attitude of mind toward those things and happenings.

The mind that is disciplined by Purity and fortified by Wisdom avoids all those lusts and desires which are inseparately bound up with affliction, and so arrives at enlightenment and peace.

To condemn others as evil, and to curse at outside conditions as the source of evil, increases and does not lessen, the world's suffering and unrest. The outer is but the shadow and effect of the inner, and when the heart is pure all outward things are pure.

All growth and life is from within outward; all decay and death is from without inward. This is the universal law. All evolution proceeds from within. All adjustment must take place within. He who ceases to strive against others, and employs his powers in the transformation, regeneration, and development of his own mind, conserves his energies and preserves himself. And as he succeeds in harmonizing his own mind, he leads others by consideration and charity into a like blessed state.

The way of enlightenment and peace is not gained by assuming authority and guidance over other minds, but by exercising a lawful authority over one's own mind, and by guiding one's self in pathways of steadfast and lofty virtue.

A man's life proceeds from his heart and his mind. He has compounded that mind by his own thoughts and deeds. It is within his power to refashion that mind by his choice of thought. In this manner he can transform his life. Let us see how this is to be done.

5

FORMATION OF HABIT

Every established mental condition is an acquired habit, and it has become such by continuous repetition of thought. Despondency and cheerfulness, anger and calmness, covetousness and generosity—indeed, all states of mind—are habits built up by choice, until they have become automatic. A thought constantly repeated at last becomes a fixed habit of the mind, and from such habits proceeds one's life.

It is in the nature of the mind to acquire knowledge by the repetition of its experiences. A thought which is very difficult, at first, to hold and dwell upon, at last becomes, by constantly being held in the mind, a natural and habitual practice.

A boy, when commencing to learn a trade, cannot even handle his tools right, much less use them correctly, but after long repetition and practice, he plies them with perfect ease and consummate skill. Likewise, a state of mind, at first apparently incapable of realization, is, by perseverance and practice, at last acquired and built into the character as a natural and spontaneous condition.

In this power of the mind to form and reform its habits, its conditions, is contained the basis of a man's salvation. It is the open door to perfect liberty by the mastery of self. For as a man has the power to form harmful habits, so he equally has the same power to create habits that are essentially good. And here we come to a point which needs some clarifying, and which calls for deep and earnest thought on the part of my reader.

It is commonly said to be easier to do wrong than right, to sin than to be holy. Such a condition has come to be regarded, almost universally, as a self-evident truth.

No less a teacher than the Buddha has said: "Bad deeds, and deeds hurtful to ourselves, are easy to do; what is beneficial and good, that is very difficult to do."

And with regards to humanity generally, this is true, but it is only true as a passing experience, a fleeting factor in human evolution. It is not a fixed condition of things. It is not the nature of an eternal truth. It is easier for men to do wrong than right, because of the prevalence of ignorance, because the true nature of things, and the essence and meaning of life, are not understood.

When a child is learning to write, it is extremely easy to hold the pen wrongly, and to form his letters incorrectly, but it is painfully difficult to hold the pen and to write properly. This is because of the child's ignorance of the art of writing, which can only be dispelled by persistent effort and practice, until, at last, it becomes natural and easy to hold the pen correctly, and difficult, as well as altogether unnecessary, to do the wrong thing.

It is the same in the vital things of mind and life. To think and do rightly requires much practice and renewed effort. But the time comes at last when it becomes habitual and easy to think and do rightly, and difficult, as it is then seen to be altogether unnecessary, to do that which is wrong.

Just as an artisan becomes, by practice, accomplished in his craft, so you can become, by practice, accomplished in goodness. It is entirely a matter of forming new habits of thought. And he to whom right thoughts have become easy and natural, and wrong thoughts and acts difficult to do, has attained to the highest virtue, to pure spiritual knowledge.

WRONG HABITS THE GATEWAY TO HELL?

It is easy and natural for men to sin because they have formed by incessant repetition, harmful and unenlightened habits of thought. It is very difficult for the thief to refrain from stealing when the opportunity occurs, because he has lived so long in covetous and greedy thoughts.

But such difficulty does not exist for the honest man who has lived so long with upright and honest thoughts. He has thereby become so enlightened as to the wrong, folly, and fruitlessness of theft, that even the remotest idea of stealing does not enter his mind. The sin of theft is a very extreme one, and I have introduced it in order to more clearly illustrate the force and formation of habit. But all sins and virtues are formed in the same way.

Anger and impatience are natural and easy to thousands of people, because they are constantly repeating angry and impatient thoughts and acts. And with each repetition the habit is more firmly established and more deeply rooted.

Calmness and patience can become habitual in the same way—by first grasping through effort, a calm and patient thought, and then continuously thinking it, and living in it, until "use becomes second nature," and anger and impatience pass away forever. It is in this manner that every wrong thought may be expelled from the mind; that every untrue act may be destroyed; that every sin may be overcome.

6

THOUGHT AND ACTION

As the fruit to the tree and the water to the spring, so is action to thought. It does not come into manifestation suddenly and without a cause. It is the result of a long and silent growth; the end of a hidden process which has long been gathering force. The fruit of the tree and the water gushing from the rock are both the effect of a combination of natural processes in air and earth which have long worked together in secret to produce the phenomenon; and the beautiful acts of enlightenment and the dark deeds of sin are both the ripened effects of trains of thought which have long been harboured in the mind.

The sudden falling, when greatly tempted, into some grievous sin by one who was believed, and who probably believed himself, to stand firm, is seen neither to be a sudden nor a causeless thing when the hidden process of thought which led up to it are revealed. The falling was merely the end, the outworking, the finished result of what commenced in the mind probably years before. The man had allowed a wrong thought to enter his mind; and a second and a third time he had welcomed it, and allowed it to nestle in his heart. Gradually he became accustomed to it, and cherished, and fondled, and tended it; and so it grew, until at last it attained such strength and force that it attracted to itself the opportunity which enabled it to burst forth and ripen into act. As falls the stately building whose foundations have been gradually undermined by the action of water, so at last falls the strong man who allows corrupt thoughts to creep into his mind and secretly undermine his character.

When it is seen that all sin and temptation are the natural outcome of the thoughts of the individual, the way to overcome sin and temptation becomes plain, and its achievement a near possibility, and, sooner or later, a certain reality; for if a man will admit, cherish, and brood upon thoughts that are pure and good, those thoughts, just as surely as the impure, will grow and gather force, and will at last attract to themselves the opportunities which will enable them to ripen into act.

HE WHO THINKS GOOD, REAPS GOOD

"There is nothing hidden that shall not be revealed," and every thought that is harboured in the mind must, by virtue of the impelling force which is inherent in the universe, at last blossom into act good or bad according to its nature. The divine Teacher and the sensualist are both the product of their own thoughts, and have become what they are as the result of the seeds of thought which they have implanted, are allowed to fall, into the garden of the heart, and have afterwards watered, tended, and cultivated.

Let no man think he can, overcome sin and temptation by wrestling with opportunity; he can only overcome them by purifying his thoughts; and if he will, day by day, in the silence of his soul, and in the performance of his duties, strenuously overcome all erroneous inclination, and put in its place thoughts that are true and that will endure the light, opportunity to do evil will give place to opportunity for accomplishing good, for a man can only attract that to him which is in harmony with his nature, and no temptation can gravitate to a man unless there is that in his heart which is capable of responding to it.

Guard well your thoughts, reader, for what you really are in your secret thoughts today, be it good or evil, you will, sooner or later, become in actual deed. He who unwearingly guards the portals of his mind against the intrusion of sinful thoughts, and occupies himself with loving thoughts, with pure, strong, and beautiful thoughts, will, when the season of their ripening comes, bring forth the fruits of gentle and holy deeds, and no temptation that can come against him shall find him unarmed or unprepared.

7

MENTAL CONDITIONS AND THEIR AFFECTS

Without going into the details of the greater steps and lessons in the right life (a task outside the scope of this small work) a few hints concerning those mental conditions from which life in its totality springs seem in order. These hints will prove helpful to those who are ready and willing to penetrate further into the inner realm of heart and mind where Love, Wisdom, and Peace await the rapidly progressing student of life.

All sin is ignorance. It is a condition of darkness and undevelopment. The wrongthinker and the wrong-doer is in the same position in the school of life as the ignorant pupil in the school of learning. He has yet to learn how to think and act correctly, that is, in accordance with Law. The pupil in learning is not happy so long as he does his lessons wrongly. Likewise, unhappiness cannot be escaped while sin remains unconquered.

Life is a series of lessons. Some are diligent in learning them, and they become pure, wise, and altogether happy. Others are negligent, and do not apply themselves. They remain impure, foolish, and unhappy.

Every form of unhappiness springs from a wrong condition of mind. Happiness is inherent in right conditions of mind. Happiness is mental harmony, unhappiness is mental inharmony. While a man lives in wrong conditions of mind, he will live a wrong life, and will suffer continually.

Suffering is rooted in error. Bliss is inherent in enlightenment. There is salvation for man only in the destruction of his own ignorance, error, and self-delusion. Where there are wrong conditions of mind there is bondage and unrest. Where there are right conditions of mind there is freedom and peace.

THE POWER OF GOOD AND EVIL

Here are some of the leading wrong mental conditions and their disastrous effects upon one's life:

1. Hatred—which leads to injury, violence, disaster, and suffering.
2. Lust—which leads to confusion of intellect, remorse, shame, and wretchedness.
3. Covetousness—which leads to fear, unrest, unhappiness, and loss.
4. Pride—which leads to disappointment, humiliation, and lack of self-knowledge.
5. Vanity—which leads to distress and mortification of spirit.
6. Condemnation—which leads to persecution and hatred from others.
7. Ill-will—which leads to failures and troubles.
8. Self-indulgence—which leads to misery, loss of judgment, grossness, disease, and neglect. 9. Anger—which leads to the loss of power and influence.
10. Desire or Self-slavery—which leads to grief, folly, sorrow, uncertainty, and loneliness.

The above wrong conditions of mind are merely negations. They are states of darkness and deprivation and not of positive power. Evil is not a power; it is ignorance and misuse of good. The hater is he who has failed to do the lesson of Love correctly, and he suffers in consequence. When he succeeds in doing it rightly, the hatred will have disappeared, and he will see and understand the darkness and impotence of hatred. This is so with every wrong condition.

The following are some of the more important right mental conditions and their beneficial effects upon one's life:

1. Love—which leads to gentle conditions, bliss, and blessedness.
2. Purity—which leads to intellectual clearness, joy, invincible confidence.
3. Selflessness—which leads to courage, satisfaction, happiness, and abundance.
4. Humility—which leads to calmness, restfulness, knowledge of Truth.
5. Gentleness—which leads to emotional equilibrium, contentment under all circumstances.
6. Compassion—which leads to protection, love, and reverence from others.
7. Goodwill—which leads to gladness, success.
8. Self-control—which leads to peace of mind, true judgment, refinement, health, and honor.
9. Patience—which leads to mental power, far-reaching influence.
10. Self-conquest—which leads to enlightenment, wisdom, insight, and profound peace.

The above right conditions of mind are states of positive power, light, joyful possession, and knowledge. The good man knows. He has learned to do his lessons correctly, and thereby understands the exact proportions which make up the sum of life. He is enlightened, and he knows good and evil. He is supremely happy, doing only that which is divinely right.

The man who is involved in the wrong conditions of mind, does not know. He is ignorant of good and evil, of himself, of the inward causes which make his life. He is unhappy, and believes other people are entirely the cause of his unhappiness. He works blindly, and lives in darkness, seeing no central purpose in existence, and no orderly and lawful sequence in the course of things.

He who aspires to the attainment of the Higher Life in its completion—who would perceive with unveiled vision the true order of things and the meaning of life—let him abandon all the wrong conditions of the heart, and persevere unceasingly in the practice of good. If he suffers, or doubts, or is unhappy, let him search within until he finds the cause, and having found it, let him cast it away. Let him so guard and purify his heart that every day less of evil and more of good shall issue therefrom. So he will daily become stronger, nobler, and wiser. So will his blessedness increase, and the Light of Truth, growing ever brighter and brighter within him, will dispel all gloom, and illuminate his Pathway.

8

LIGHT ON GOOD MANNERS AND REFINEMENT

More upward, working out the beast, And let the ape and tiger die.

All culture is getting AWAY from the beast. Evolution is a refining process, and the unwritten laws of society are inherent in the evolutionary law.

Education is intellectual culture. The scholar is engaged in purifying and perfecting his intellect; the spiritual devotee is engaged in purifying and perfecting his heart.

When a man aspires to nobler heights of achievement, and sets about the realization of his ideal, he commences to refine his nature; and the more pure a man makes himself within, the more refined, gracious, and gentle will be his outward demeanor.

Good manners have an ethical basis, and cannot be divorced from religion. To be illmannered is to be imperfect, for what are ill manners but the outward expression of inward defects? What a man does, that he is. If he acts rudely, he is a rude man; if he acts foolishly, he is a foolish man; if he acts gently, he is a gentleman. It is a mistake to suppose that a man can have a gentle and refined mind behind a rough and brutal exterior (though such a man may possess some strong animal virtues), as the outer is an expression of the inner.

THE BUDDHIST WAY OF LIFE

One of the steps in the noble Eightfold Path to perfection as expounded by Buddha is—Right Conduct or Good Behavior. It should be plain to all that the man who has not yet learned how to conduct himself toward others in a kindly, gracious, and unselfish spirit has not yet entered the pathway of the holy life.

If a man refines his heart, he will refine his behavior; if he refines his behavior, it will help him to refine his heart.

To be coarse, brutish, and snappish may be natural to the beast, but the man who aspires to be even an endurable member of society (not to mention the higher manhood), will at once purge away any such bestial traits that may possess him.

All these things which aid in man's refinement—such as music, painting, poetry, manners—are servants and messengers of progress. Man degrades himself when he imitates the brute. Let us not mistake barbarism for simplicity or vulgarity for honesty.

Unselfishness, kindliness, and consideration for others will always be manifested outwardly as gentleness, graciousness, and refinement. To affect these graces by simulating them may seem to succeed, but it does not. Affectation and hypocrisy are soon divulged; every man's eye, sooner or later, pierces through their flimsiness, and ultimately none but the actors of them are deceived. As Emerson says:

"What is done for effect, is seen to be done for effect; and what is done for love, is felt to be done for love."

Children who are well-bred are taught always to consider the happiness of others before their own: to offer others the most comfortable seat, the choicest fruit, the best tidbit, and so on, and also to do everything, even the most trivial acts, in the right way. And these two things—unselfishness and right action—are at the basis, not only of good manners, but of all ethics, religion, and true living; they represent power and skill. The selfish man is weak and unskillful in his actions. Unselfishness is the right way of thinking; good manners are the right way of acting, As Emerson, again, says:

"There is always a way of doing everything, if it be to boil an egg. Manners are the happy way of doing things right."

It is a frequent error among men to imagine that the Higher Life is an ideal something quite above and apart from the common details of life, and that to neglect these or to perform them in a slovenly manner is an indication that the mind is preoccupied on "higher things." Whereas it is an indication that the mind is becoming inexact, dreamy, and weak, instead of exact, wide awake, and strong. No matter how apparently trivial the thing is which has to be done, there is a right way of doing it, and to do it in the right way saves friction, time, and trouble, conserves power, and develops grace, skill, and happiness.

The artisan has a variety of tools with which to ply his particular craft, and he is taught (and also finds by experience) that each tool must be applied to its special use, and never under any circumstances must one tool be made to do service for another. By using every tool in its proper place and in the right way, the maximum of dexterity and power is attained. Should a boy learning a trade refuse instruction, and persist in using the tools in his own way, making one tool do service for another, he would never become anything better than a clumsy bungler, and would be a failure in his trade.

It is the same throughout the whole life. If a man opens himself to receive instruction, and studies how to do everything rightly and lawfully, he becomes strong, skillful, and wise, master of himself, his thoughts and actions. But if he persists in following his momentary impulses, in doing everything as he feels prompted, not exercising thoughtfulness, and rejecting instruction, such a man will attain to nothing better than a slovenly and bungling life.

Confucius paid the strictest attention to dress, eating, deportment, passing speech—to all the so-called trivialities of life, as well as to the momentous affairs of state and the lofty moral principles which he expounded. He taught his disciples that it is the sign of a vulgar and foolish mind to regard anything as "trivial" that is necessary to be done, that the wise man pays attention to all his duties, and does everything wisely, thoughtfully, and rightly.

It is not an arbitrary edict of society that the man who persists in eating with his knife be rejected, for a knife is given to cut with, and a fork to eat with, and to put things to wrong and slovenly uses—even in the passing details of life—does not make for progress, but is retrogressive and makes for confusion.

It is not a despotic condition in the law of things that so long as a man persists in thinking and acting unkindly toward others he shall be shut out from Heaven. He shall remain in the outer pain and unrest, for selfishness is disruption and disorder. The universe is sustained by exactness, it rests on order, it demands right doing, and the searcher of wisdom will watch all his ways. He will think purely, speak gently, and act graciously, refining his entire nature, both in the letter and the spirit.

9

THE ORIGINAL SIMPLICITY

Life is simple. Being is simple. The universe is simple. Complexity arises in ignorance and self-delusion. The "Original Simplicity" of Lao-tze is a term expressive of the universe as it is, and not as it appears. Looking through the woven network of his own illusions, man sees interminable complication and unfathomable mystery, and so loses himself in the labyrinths of his own making. Let a man put away egotism, and he will see the universe in all the beauty of its pristine simplicity. Let him annihilate the delusion of the personal "I," and he will destroy all the illusions which spring from that "I." He will thus "re-become a little child," and will "revert to Original Simplicity."

When a man succeeds in entirely forgetting (annihilating) his personal self, he be-comes a mirror in which the universal Reality is faultlessly reflected. He is awakened, and henceforward he lives, not in dreams, but realities.

Pythagoras saw the universe in the ten numbers, but even this simplicity may be further reduced, and the universe ultimately be found to be contained in the number ONE, for all the numerals and all their infinite complications are but additions of the One.

Let life cease to be lived as a fragmentary thing, and let it be lived as a perfect Whole; the simplicity of the Perfect will then be revealed.

How shall the fragment comprehend the Whole? Yet how simple that the Whole should comprehend the fragment. How shall sin perceive Holiness? Yet how plain that Holiness should understand sin. He who would become the Greater let him abandon the lesser. In no form is the circle contained, but in the circle all forms are contained. In no colour is the radiant light imprisoned, but in the radiant light all colours are embodied, Let a man destroy all the forms of self, and he shall apprehend the Circle of Perfection; let him submerge, in the silent depths of his being, the varying colours of his thoughts and desires, and he shall be illuminated with the White Light of Divine Knowledge. In the perfect chord of music the single note, though forgotten, is indispensably contained, and the drop of water becomes of supreme usefulness by losing itself in the ocean. Sink thyself compassionately in the heart of humanity, and thou shalt reproduce the harmonies of Heaven; lose thyself in unlimited love toward all, and thou shalt work enduring works and shalt become one with the eternal Ocean of Bliss.

Man evolves outward to the periphery of complexity, and then involves backward to the Central Simplicity. When a man discovers that it is mathematically impossible for him to know the universe before knowing himself, he then starts upon the Way which leads to the Original Simplicity. He begins to unfold from within, and as he Unfolds himself, he enfolds the universe.

Cease to speculate about God, and find the all-embracing Good within thee, then shalt thou see the emptiness and vanity of speculation, knowing thyself one with God.

He who will not give up his secret lust, his covetousness, his anger, his opinion about this or that, can see nor know nothing; he will remain a dullard in the school of Wisdom, though he be accounted learned in the colleges.

If a man would find the Key of Knowledge, let him find himself. Thy sins are not thyself; they are not any part of thyself;

they are diseases which thou hast come to love. Cease to cling to them, and they will no longer cling to thee. Let them fall away, and thy self shall stand revealed. Thou shalt then know thyself as Comprehensive Vision, Invincible Principle, Immortal Life, and Eternal Good.

GOODNESS FOLLOWS SIMPLICITY

The impure man believes impurity to be his rightful condition, but the pure man knows himself as pure being; he also, penetrating the Veils, sees all others as pure being. Purity is extremely simple, and needs no argument to support it; impurity is interminably complex, and is ever involved in defensive argument. Truth lives itself. A blameless life is the only witness of Truth. Men cannot see, and will not accept the witness until they find it within themselves; and having found it, a man becomes silent before his fellows. Truth is so simple that it cannot be found in the region of argument and advertisement, and so silent that it is only manifested in actions.

So extremely simple is Original Simplicity, that a man must let go his hold of everything before he can perceive it. The great arch is strong by virtue of the hollowness underneath, and a wise man becomes strong and invincible by emptying himself.

Meekness, Patience, Love, Compassion, and Wisdom—these are the dominant qualities of Original Simplicity; therefore the imperfect cannot understand it. Wisdom only can apprehend Wisdom, therefore the fool says, "No man is wise." The imperfect man says, "No man can be perfect," and he therefore remains where he is. Though he live with a perfect man all his life, he shall not behold his perfection. Meekness he will call cowardice; Patience, Love, and Compassion he will see as weakness; and Wisdom will appear to him as folly. Faultless discrimination belongs to the Perfect Whole, and resides not in any part, therefore men are exhorted to refrain from judgement until they have themselves manifested the Perfect Life.

Arriving at Original Simplicity, opacity disappears, and the universal transparency becomes apparent. He who has found the indwelling Reality of his own being has found the original and universal Reality. Knowing the Divine Heart within, all hearts are known, and the thoughts of all men become his who has become the master of his own thoughts; therefore the good man does not defend himself, but moulds the minds of others to his own likeness.

As the problematical transcends crudity, so Pure Goodness transcends the problematical. All problems vanish when Pure Goodness is reached; therefore the good man is called "The slayer of illusions." What problem can vex where sin is not? O thou who strivest loudly and restest not! retire into the holy silence of thine own being, and live therefrom. So shalt thou, finding Pure Goodness, rend in twain the Veil of the Temple of Illusion, and shalt enter into the Patience, Peace, and transcendent Glory of the Perfect, for Pure Goodness and Original Simplicity are one.

10

THE SECRET OF HEALTH, SUCCESS AND POWER

We all remember with what intense delight, as children, we listened to the nevertiring fairy-tale. How eagerly we followed the fluctuating fortunes of the good boy or girl, ever protected, in the hour of crisis, from the evil machinations of the scheming witch, the cruel giant, or the wicked king.

And our little hearts never faltered for the fate of the hero or heroine, nor did we doubt their ultimate triumph over all their enemies, for we knew that the fairies were infallible, and that they would never desert those who had consecrated themselves to the good and the true.

And what unspeakable joy pulsated within us when the Fairy-Queen, bringing all her magic to bear at the critical moment, scattered all the darkness and trouble, and granted them the complete satisfaction of all their hopes, and they were "happy ever after."

With the accumulating years, and an ever-increasing intimacy with the so-called "realities" of life, our beautiful fairy-world became obliterated, and its wonderful inhabitants were relegated, in the archives of memory, to the shadowy and unreal.

And we thought we were wise and strong in thus leaving for ever the land of childish dreams, but as we re-become little children in the wondrous world of wisdom, we shall return again to the inspiring dreams of childhood and find that they are, after all, realities.

The fairy-folk, so small and nearly always invisible, yet possessed of an all-conquering and magical power, who bestow upon the good, health, wealth, and happiness, along with all the gifts of nature in lavish profusion, start again into reality and become immortalized in the soul-realm of him who, by growth in wisdom, has entered into a knowledge of the power of thought, and the laws which govern the inner world of being.

To him the fairies live again as thought-people, thought-messengers, thoughtpowers working in harmony with the over-ruling Good. And they who, day by day, endeavor to harmonize their hearts with the heart of the Supreme Good, do in reality acquire true health, wealth, and happiness.

There is no protection to compare with goodness, and by "goodness" I do not mean a mere outward conformity to the rules of morality; I mean pure thought, noble aspiration, unselfish love, and freedom from vainglory.

To dwell continually in good thoughts, is to throw around oneself a psychic atmosphere of sweetness and power which leaves its impress upon all who come in contact with it.

As the rising sun puts to rout the helpless shadows, so are all the impotent forces of evil put to flight by the searching rays of positive thought which shine forth from a heart made strong in purity and faith.

Where there is sterling faith and uncompromising purity there is health, there is success, there is power. In such a one, disease, failure, and disaster can find no lodgment, for there is nothing on which they can feed.

Even physical conditions are largely determined by mental states, and to this truth the scientific world is rapidly being drawn.

HEALTH IS WEALTH

The old, materialistic belief that a man is what his body makes him, is rapidly passing away, and is being replaced by the inspiring belief that man is superior to his body, and that his body is what he makes it by the power of thought.

Men everywhere are ceasing to believe that a man is despairing because he is dyspeptic, and are coming to understand that he is dyspeptic because he is despairing, and in the near future, the fact that all disease has its origin in the mind will become common knowledge.

There is no evil in the universe but has its root and origin in the mind, and sin, sickness, sorrow, and affliction do not, in reality, belong to the universal order, are not inherent in the nature of things, but are the direct outcome of our ignorance of the right relations of things.

According to tradition, there once lived, in India, a school of philosophers who led a life of such absolute purity and simplicity that they commonly reached the age of one hundred and fifty years, and to fall sick was looked upon by them as an unpardonable disgrace, for it was considered to indicate a violation of law.

The sooner we realize and acknowledge that sickness, far from being the arbitrary visitation of an offended God, or the test of an unwise Providence, is the result of our own error or sin, the sooner shall we enter upon the highway of health.

Disease comes to those who attract it, to those whose minds and bodies are receptive to it, and flees from those whose strong, pure, and positive thought-sphere generates healing and life-giving currents.

If you are given to anger, worry, jealousy, greed, or any other inharmonious state of mind, and expect perfect physical health, you are expecting the impossible, for you are continually sowing the seeds of disease in your mind.

Such conditions of mind are carefully shunned by the wise man, for he knows them to be far more dangerous than a bad drain or an infected house.

If you would be free from all physical aches and pains, and would enjoy perfect physical harmony, then put your mind in order, and harmonize your thoughts. Think joyful thoughts; think loving thoughts; let the elixir of goodwill course through your veins, and you will need no other medicine. Put away your jealousies, your suspicions, your worries, your hatreds, your selfish indulgences, and you will put away your dyspepsia, your biliousness, your nervousness and aching joints.

If you will persist in clinging to these debilitating and demoralizing habits of mind, then do not complain when your body is laid low with sickness. The following story illustrates the close relation that exists between habits of mind and bodily conditions.

A certain man was afflicted with a painful disease, and he tried one physician after another, but all to no purpose. He then visited towns which were famous for their curative waters, and after having bathed in them all, his disease was more painful than ever.

One night he dreamed that a Presence came to him and said, "Brother, hast thou tried all the means of cure?" and he replied, "I have tried all." "Nay," said the Presence, "Come with me, and I will show thee a healing bath which has escaped thy notice."

The afflicted man followed, and the Presence led him to a clear pool of water, and said, "Plunge thyself in this water and thou shalt surely recover," and thereupon vanished.

The man plunged into the water, and on coming out, Io! his disease had left him, and at the same moment he saw written above the pool the word "Renounce." Upon waking, the fall meaning of his dream flashed across his mind, and looking within he discovered that he had, all along, been a victim to a sinful indulgence, and he vowed that he would renounce it for ever.

He carried out his vow, and from that day his affliction began to leave him, and in a short time he was completely restored to health. Many people complain that they have broken down through over-work. In the majority of such cases the breakdown is more frequently the result of foolishly wasted energy.

If you would secure health you must learn to work without friction. To become anxious or excited, or to worry over needless details is to invite a breakdown.

Work, whether of brain or body, is beneficial and health-giving, and the man who can work with a steady and calm persistency, freed from all anxiety and worry, and with his mind utterly oblivious to all but the work he has in hand, will not only accomplish far more than the man who is always hurried and anxious, but he will retain his health, a boon which the other quickly forfeits.

True health and true success go together, for they are inseparably intertwined in the thought-realm. As mental harmony produces bodily health, so it also leads to a harmonious sequence in the actual working out of one's plans.

THE MIGHT OF FAITH

Order your thoughts and you will order your life. Pour the oil of tranquility upon the turbulent waters of the passions and prejudices, and the tempests of misfortune, howsoever they may threaten, will be powerless to wreck the barque of your soul, as it threads its way across the ocean of life.

And if that barque be piloted by a cheerful and never-failing faith its course will be doubly sure, and many perils will pass it by which would other-wise attack it.

By the power of faith every enduring work is accomplished.

Faith in the Supreme; faith in the over-ruling Law; faith in your work, and in your power to accomplish that work, -here is the rock upon which you must build if you would achieve, if you would stand and not fall.

To follow, under all circumstances, the highest promptings within you; to be always true to the divine self; to rely upon the inward Light, the inward Voice, and to pursue your purpose with a fearless and restful heart, believing that the future will yield unto you the meed of every thought and effort; knowing that the laws of the universe can never fail, and that your own will come back to you with mathematical exactitude, this is faith and the living of faith.

By the power of such a faith the dark waters of uncertainty are divided, every mountain of difficulty crumbles away, and the believing soul passes on unharmed.

Strive, O reader! to acquire, above everything, the priceless possession of this dauntless faith, for it is the talisman of happiness, of success, of peace, of power, of all that makes life great and superior to suffering.

Build upon such a faith, and you build upon the Rock of the Eternal, and with the materials of the Eternal, and the structure that you erect will never be dissolved, for it will transcend all the accumulations of material luxuries and riches, the end of which is dust.

Whether you are hurled into the depths of sorrow or lifted upon the heights of joy, ever retain your hold upon this faith, ever return to it as your rock of refuge, and keep your feet firmly planted upon its immortal and immovable base.

Centered in such a faith, you will become possessed of such a spiritual strength as will shatter, like so many toys of glass, all the forces of evil that are hurled against you, and you will achieve a success such as the mere striver after worldly gain can never know or even dream of. "If ye have faith, and doubt not, ye shall not only do this, ... but if ye shall say unto this mountain, be thou removed and be thou cast into the sea, it shall be done."

There are those today, men and women tabernacled in flesh and blood, who have realized this faith, who live in it and by it day by day, and who, having put it to the uttermost test, have entered into the possession of its glory and peace.

Such have sent out the word of command, and the mountains of sorrow and disappointment, of mental weariness and physical pain have passed from them, and have been cast into the sea of oblivion.

If you will become possessed of this faith you will not need to trouble about your success or failure, and success will come.

You will not need to become anxious about results, but will work joyfully and peacefully, knowing that right thoughts and right efforts will inevitably bring about right results.

I know a lady who has entered into many blissful satisfactions, and recently a friend remarked to her, "Oh, how fortunate you are! You only have to wish for a thing, and it comes to you."

And it did, indeed, appear so on the surface; but in reality all the blessedness that has entered into this woman's life is the direct outcome of the inward state of blessedness which she has, throughout life, been cultivating and training toward perfection.

Mere wishing brings nothing but disappointment; it is living that tells.

The foolish wish and grumble; the wise, work and wait. And this woman had worked; worked without and within, but especially within upon heart and soul; and with the invisible hands of the spirit she had built up, with the precious stones of faith, hope, joy, devotion, and love, a fair temple of light, whose glorifying radiance was ever round about her.

It beamed in her eye; it shone through her countenance; it

vibrated in her voice; and all who came into her presence felt its captivating spell.

And as with her, so with you. Your success, your failure, your influence, your whole life you carry about with you, for your dominant trends of thought are the determining factors in your destiny.

Send forth loving, stainless, and happy thoughts, and blessings will fall into your hands, and your table will be spread with the cloth of peace.

Send forth hateful, impure, and unhappy thoughts, and curses will rain down upon you, and fear and unrest will wait upon your pillow. You are the unconditional maker of your fate, be that fate what it may. Every moment you are sending forth from you the influences which will make or mar your life.

Let your heart grow large and loving and unselfish, and great and lasting will be your influence and success, even though you make little money.

Confine it within the narrow limits of self-interest, and even though you become a millionaire your influence and success, at the final reckoning will be found to be utterly insignificant. Cultivate, then, this pure and unselfish spirit, and combine with purity and faith, singleness of purpose, and you are evolving from within the elements, not only of abounding health and enduring success, but of greatness and power.

THE PROFESSIONAL CODE OF ETHICS

If your present position is distasteful to you, and your heart is not in your work, nevertheless perform your duties with scrupulous diligence, and whilst resting your mind in the idea that the better position and greater opportunities are waiting for you, ever keep an active mental outlook for budding possibilities, so that when the critical moment arrives, and the new channel presents itself, you will step into it with your mind fully prepared for the undertaking, and with that intelligence and foresight which is born of mental discipline.

Whatever your task may be, concentrate your whole mind upon it, throw into it all the energy of which you are capable. The faultless completion of small tasks leads inevitably to larger tasks. See to it that you rise by steady climbing, and you will never fall. And herein lies the secret of true power.

Learn, by constant practice, how to husband your resources, and to concentrate them, at any moment, upon a given point. The foolish waste all their mental and spiritual energy in frivolity, foolish chatter, or selfish argument, not to mention wasteful physical excesses.

If you would acquire overcoming power you must cultivate poise and passivity. You must be able to stand alone. All power is associated with immovability. The mountain, the massive rock, the storm-tried oak, all speak to us of power, because of their combined solitary grandeur and defiant fixity; while the shifting sand, the yielding twig, and the waving reed speak to us of weakness, because they are movable and non-resistant, and are utterly useless when detached from their fellows.

He is the man of power who, when all his fellows are swayed by some emotion or passion, remains calm and unmoved. He only is fitted to command and control who has succeeded in commanding and controlling himself.

The hysterical, the fearful, the thoughtless and frivolous, let such seek company, or they will fall for lack of support; but the calm, the fearless, the thoughtful, and let such seek the solitude of the forest, the desert, and the mountain-top, and to their power more power will be added, and they will more and more successfully stem the psychic currents and whirlpools which engulf mankind.

Passion is not power; it is the abuse of power, the dispersion of power. Passion is like a furious storm which beats fiercely and wildly upon the embattled rock whilst power is like the rock itself, which remains silent and unmoved through it all.

That was a manifestation of true power when Martin Luther, wearied with the persuasions of his fearful friends, who were doubtful as to his safety should he go to Worms, replied, "If there were as many devils in Worms as there are tiles on the housetops I would go."

And when Benjamin Disraeli broke down in his first Parliamentary speech, and brought upon himself the derision of the House, that was an exhibition of germinal power when he exclaimed, "The day will come when you will consider it an honor to listen to me."

When that young man, whom I knew, passing through continual reverses and misfortunes, was mocked by his friends and told to desist from further effort, and he replied, "The time is not far distant when you will marvel at my good fortune and success," he showed that he was possessed of that silent and irresistible power which has taken him over innumerable difficulties, and crowned his life with success.

If you have not this power, you may acquire it by practice, and the beginning of power is likewise the beginning of wisdom. You must commence by overcoming those purposeless trivialities to which you have hitherto been a willing victim.

Boisterous and uncontrolled laughter, slander and idle talk, and joking merely to raise a laugh, all these things must be put on one side as so much waste of valuable energy.

St. Paul never showed his wonderful insight into the hidden laws of human progress to greater advantage than when he warned the Ephesians against "Foolish talking and jesting which is not convenient," for to dwell habitually in such practices is to destroy all spiritual power and life.

As you succeed in rendering yourself impervious to such mental dissipations you will begin to understand what true power is, and you will then commence to grapple with the more powerful desires and appetites which hold your soul in bondage, and bar the way to power, and your further progress will then be made clear.

Above all be of single aim; have a legitimate and useful purpose, and devote yourself unreservedly to it. Let nothing draw you aside ; remember that the doubleminded man is unstable in all his ways.

Be eager to learn, but slow to beg. Have a thorough understanding of your work, and let it be your own; and as you proceed, ever following the inward Guide, the infallible Voice, you will pass on from victory to victory, and will rise step by step to higher resting-places, and your ever-broadening outlook will gradually reveal to you the essential beauty and purpose of life.

Self-purified, health will be yours; faith-protected, success will be yours; self-governed, power will be yours, and all that you do will prosper, for, ceasing to be a disjointed unit, self-enslaved, you will be in harmony with the Great Law, working no longer against, but with, the Universal Life, the Eternal Good.

And what health you gain it will remain with you; what success you achieve will be beyond all human computation, and will never pass away; and what influence and power you wield will continue to increase throughout the ages, for it will be a part of that unchangeable Principle which supports the universe.

This, then, is the secret of health,—a pure heart and a well-ordered mind; this is the secret of success,—an unfaltering faith, and a wisely-directed purpose; and to rein in, with unfaltering will, the dark steed of desire, this is the secret of power.

All ways are waiting for my feet to tread,
The light and dark, the living and the dead,
The broad and narrow way, the high and low,

The good and bad, and with quick step or slow,
I now may enter any way I will,
And find, by walking, which is good, which ill.

And all good things my wandering feet await,
If I but come, with vow inviolate,
Unto the narrow, high and holy way
Of heart-born purity, and therein stay;
Walking, secure from him who taunts and scorns,
To flowery meads, across the path of thorns.

And I may stand where health, success, and power
Await my coming, if, each fleeting hour,
I cling to love and patience; and abide
With stainlessness; and never step aside
From high integrity ; so shall I see
At last the land of immortality.

And I may seek and find; I may achieve,
I may not claim, but, losing, may retrieve.
The law bends not for me, but I must bend
Unto the law, if I would reach the end
Of my afflictions, if I would restore
My soul to Light and Life, and weep no more.

Not mine the arrogant and selfish claim
To all good things; be mine the lowly aim
To seek and find, to know and comprehend,
And wisdom-ward all holy footsteps wend,
Nothing is mine to claim or to command,
But all is mine to know and understand.

11

SMALL TASKS AND DUTIES

"Wrapped in our nearest duty is the key
Which shall unlock for us the Heavenly Gate:
Unveiled, the Heavenly Vision he shall see,
Who cometh not too early nor too late."

"Like the star
That shines afar,
Without haste
And without rest,

Let each man wheel with steady sway
Round the task that rules the day,
And do his best."

—Goethe

As pain and bliss inevitably follow on wrong and right beginnings, so unhappiness and blessedness are inseparably bound up with small tasks and duties. Not that a duty has any power of itself to bestow happiness or the reverse—this is contained in the attitude of the mind which is assumed towards the duty—and everything depends upon the way in which it is approached and done.

Not only great happiness but great power arises from doing little things unselfishly, wisely, and perfectly, for life in its totality is made up of little things. Wisdom inheres in the common details of everyday existence, and when the *parts* are made perfect the *Whole* will be without blemish.

Everything in the universe is made up of little things, and the perfection of the great is based upon the perfection of the small. If any detail of the universe were imperfect the Whole would be imperfect. If any particle were omitted the aggregate would cease to be. Without a grain of dust there could be no world, and the world is perfect because the grain of dust is perfect. Neglect of the small is confusion of the great. The snowflake is as perfect as the star; the dew drop is as symmetrical as the planet; the microbe is not less mathematically proportioned than the man. By laying stone upon stone, plumbing and fitting each with perfect adjustment, the temple at last stands forth in all its architectural beauty. The small precedes the great. The small is not merely the apologetic attendant of the great, it is its master and informing genius.

Vain men are ambitious to be great, and look about to do some great thing, ignoring and despising the little tasks which call for immediate attention, and in the doing of which there is no vainglory, regarding such "trivialities" as beneath the notice of great men. The fool lacks knowledge because he lacks humility, and, inflated with the thought of self-importance, he aims at impossible things.

The great man has become such by the scrupulous and unselfish attention which he has given to small duties. He has become wise and powerful by sacrificing ambition and pride in the doing of those necessary things which evoke no applause and promise no reward. He never sought greatness; he sought faithfulness, unselfishness, integrity, truth; and in finding these in the common round of small tasks and duties he unconsciously ascended to the level of greatness.

The great man knows the vast value that inheres in moments, words, greetings, meals, apparel, correspondence, rest, work, detached efforts, fleeting obligations, in the thousand-and-one little things which press upon him for attention—briefly, in the common details of life. He sees everything as divinely apportioned, needing only the application of dispassionate thought and action on his part to render life blessed and perfect. He neglects nothing; does not hurry; seeks to escape nothing but error and folly; attends to every duty as it is presented to him, and does not postpone and regret. By giving himself unreservedly to his nearest duty, forgetting alike pleasure and pain, he attains to that combined childlike simplicity and unconscious power which is greatness.

The advice of Confucius to his disciples: "Eat at your own table as you would at the table of a king," emphasises the immeasurable importance of little things, as also does that aphorism of another great teacher, Buddha: "If anything is to be done, let a man do it, let him attack it vigorously." To neglect small tasks, or to execute them in a perfunctory or slovenly manner, is a mark of weakness and folly.

The giving of one's entire and unselfish attention to every duty in its proper place evolves, by a natural growth, higher and ever higher combinations of duties, because it evolves power and develops talent, genius, goodness, character. A man ascends into greatness as naturally and unconsciously as the plant evolves a flower, and in the same manner, by fitting, with unabated energy and diligence, every effort and detail in its proper place, thus harmonising his life and character without friction or waste of power.

Of the almost innumerable recipes for the development of "will-power" and "concentration" which are now scattered abroad, one looks almost in vain for any wholesome hint applicable to vital experience. "Breathings," "postures," "visualisings," "occult methods" are practices as delusive as they are artificial and remote from all that is real and essential in life; while the true path—the path of duty, of earnest and undivided application to one's daily task—along which alone will-power and concentration of thought can be wholesomely and normally developed, remains unknown, untrodden, unexplored even by the elect.

All unnatural forcing and straining in order to gain "power" should be abandoned. There is no way from childhood to manhood but by growth; nor is there any other way from folly to wisdom, from ignorance to knowledge, from weakness to strength. A man must learn how to grow little by little and day after day, by adding thought to thought, effort to effort, deed to deed.

It is true the fakir gains some sort of power by his long persistence in "postures" and "mortifications," but it is a power which is bought at a heavy price, and that price is an equal loss of strength in another direction. He is never a strong, useful character, but a mere fantastic specialist in some psychological trick. He is not a developed man, he is a maimed man.

True will-power consists in overcoming the irritabilities, follies, rash impulses and moral lapses which accompany the daily life of the individual, and which are apt to manifest themselves on every slight provocation; and in developing calmness, self-possession, and dispassionate action in the press and heat of worldly duties, and in the midst of the passionate and unbalanced throng. Anything short of this is not true power, and this can only be developed along the normal pathway of steady growth in executing ever more and more masterfully, unselfishly, and perfectly the daily round of legitimate tasks and pressing obligations.

The master is not he whose "psychological accomplishments," rounded by mystery and wonder, leave him in unguarded moments the prey of irritability, of regret, of peevishness, or other petty folly or vice, but he whose "mastery" is manifested in fortitude, non-resentment, steadfastness, calmness, and infinite patience. The true Master is master of himself; anything other than this is not mastery but delusion. The man who sets his whole mind on the doing of each task as it is presented, who puts into it energy and intelligence, shutting all else out from his mind, and striving to do that one thing, no matter how small, completely and perfectly, detaching himself from all reward in his task—that man will every day be acquiring greater command over his mind, and will, by ever-ascending degrees, become at last a man of power—a Master.

Put yourself unreservedly into your present task, and so work, so act, so live that you shall leave each task a finished piece of labour—this is the true way to the acquisition of will-power, concentration of thought, and conservation of energy. Look not about for magical formulas, for strained and artificial methods. Every resource is already with you and within you. You have but to learn how wisely to apply yourself in that place which you now occupy. Until this is done those other and higher places which are waiting for you cannot be taken possession of, cannot be reached.

There is no way to strength and wisdom but by acting strongly and wisely in the present moment, and each present moment reveals its own task. The great man, the wise man does small things greatly regarding nothing as "trivial" that is necessary. The weak man, the foolish man, does small things carelessly, and meanly, hankering the while after, some greater work for which, in his neglect and inability in small matters, he is ceaselessly advertising his incapacity. The man who leasts governs himself is always more ambitious to govern others and assume important responsibilities. "Who so neglects a thing which he suspects he ought to do because it seems too small a thing is deceiving himself; it is not too little but too great for him that he doeth it not."

And just as the strong doing of small tasks leads to greater strength, so the doing of those tasks weakly leads to greater weakness. What a man is in his fractional duties that he is in the aggregate of his character. Weakness is as great a source of suffering as sin, and there can be no true blessedness until some measure of strength of character is evolved. The weak man becomes strong by attaching value to little things and doing them accordingly. The strong man becomes weak by falling into looseness and neglect concerning small things, thereby forfeiting his simple wisdom and squandering his energy. Herein we see the beneficent operation of that law of growth which is expressed in the little understood words: "To him that hath shall be given, and from him that hath not shall be taken away even that which he hath." Man instantly gains or loses by every thought he thinks, every word he says, every act he does, and every work to which he puts hand and heart. His character from moment to moment is a graduating quantity, to or from which some measure of good is added or subtracted during every moment, and the gain or loss is involved, even to absoluteness, in each thought, word, and deed as these follow each other in rapid sequence.

He who masters the small becomes the rightful possessor of the great. He who is mastered by the small can achieve no superlative victory.

Life is a kind of cooperative trust in which the whole is of the nature of, and dependent upon, the unit.

A successful business, a perfect machine, a glorious temple, or a beautiful character is evolved from the perfect adjustment of a multliplicity of parts.

The foolish man thinks that little faults, little indulgences, little sins, are of no consequence; he persuades himself that so long as he does not commit flagrant immoralities he is virtuous, and even holy; but he is thereby deprived of virtue, and holiness, and the world knows him accordingly; it does not reverence, adore, and love him; it passes him by; he is reckoned of no account; his influence is destroyed. The efforts of such a man to make the world virtuous, his exhortations to his fellow-men to abandon great vices, are empty of substance and barren of fruitage. The insignificance which he attaches to his small vices permeates his whole character and is the measure of his manhood: he is regarded as an insignificant man. The levity with which he commits his errors and publishes his weakness comes back to him in the form of neglect and loss of influence and respect: he is not sought after, for who will seek to be taught of folly? His work does not prosper, for who will lean upon a reed? His words fall upon deaf ears, for they are void of practice, wisdom, and experience, and who will go after an echo?

The wise man, or he who is becoming wise, sees the danger which lurks in those common personal faults which men mostly commit thoughtlessly and with impunity; he also sees the salvation which inheres in the abandonment of those faults, as well as in the practice of virtuous thoughts and acts which the majority disregard as unimportant, and in those quiet but momentous daily conquests over self which are hidden from other's eyes.

He who regards his molest delinquencies as of the gravest nature becomes a saint. He sees the far reaching influence, good or bad, which extends from his every thought and act, and how he himself is made or unmade by the soundness or unsoundness of those innumerable details of conduct which combine to form his character and life, and so he watches, guards, purifies, and perfects himself little by little and step by step.

As the ocean is composed of drops, the earth of grains, and the stars of points of light, so is life composed of thoughts and acts; without these, life would not be. Every man's life, therefore, is what his apparently detached thoughts and acts make it. There combination is himself. As the year consists, of a given number of sequential moments, so a man's character and life consists of a given number of sequential thoughts and deeds, and the finished whole will bear the impress of the parts.

"All sorts of things and weather
Must be taken in together,
To make up a year
And a sphere."

Little kindnesses, generosities, and sacrifices make up a kind and generous character. Little renounciations, endurances, and victories over self make up a strong and noble character. The truly honest man is honest in the minutest details of his life. The noble man is noble in every little thing he says and does.

It is a fatal delusion with men to think that life is detached from the momentary thought and act, and not to understand that the passing thought and deed is the foundation and substance of life. When this is fully understood all things are seen as sacred, and every act becomes religious. Truth is wrapped up in infinitesimal details. Thoroughness is genius.

"Possessions vanish, and opinions change,
And passions hold a fluctuating seat:
But, by the storms of circumstance unshaken,
And subject neither to eclipse nor wane,
Duty exists."

You do not live your life in the mass; you live it in the fragments and from these the mass emerges. You can will to live each fragment nobly if you choose, and, this being done, there can be no particle of baseness in the finished whole. The saying "Take care of the pence and the pounds will take care of themselves" is seen to be more than worldly-wise when applied spiritually, for, to take care of the present, passing act, knowing that by so doing the total sum and amount of life and character will be safely preserved, is to be divinely wise. Do not long to do great and laudable things; these will do themselves if you do your present task nobly. Do not chafe at the restrictions and limitations of your present duty but be nobly unselfish in the doing of it, putting aside discontent, listlessness, and the foolish contemplation of great deeds which lie beyond you—and lo! already the greatness for which you sighed begins to appear. There is no weakness like peevishness. Aspire to the attainment of inward nobility, not outward glory, and begin to attain it where you now are.

The irksomeness and sting which you feel to be in your task are in your mind only. Alter your attitude of mind towards it, and at once the crooked path is made straight, the unhappiness is turned into joy.

See that your every fleeting moment is strong, pure, and purposeful; put earnestness and unselfishness into every passing task and duty; make your every thought, word, and deed sweet and true; thus learning, by practice and experience, the inestimable value of the small things of life, you will gather, little by little, abundant and enduring blessedness.

12

LIGHT ON LIFE'S CHANGES

The tendency of things to advance from a lower to a higher level, and from high to higher still, is universal. The worlds exist in order that beings may experience, and by experiencing, acquire knowledge and increase in wisdom.

Evolution is only another name for progress. It signifies perpetual change, but a purposeful change, a change accompanied by growth. Evolution does not mean the creation of a new being from a being of a different order. It means the modification of beings by experience and change; and such modification is progress.

The fact of change is ever before us. Nothing can escape it. Plants, animals, and human beings germinate, reach maturity, and pass into decay. Even the lordly suns and their attendant worlds rolling through illimitable spaces, although their life is reckoned in millions of years, at last decay and perish after having passed through innumerable changes. We cannot say of any being or object—"This will remain forever as it is," for even while we are saying it, the being or object would be undergoing change.

Sadness and suffering accompany this change; and beings mourn for that which has departed, for the things which are lost and gone. Yet in reality change is good, for it is the open door to all achievement, advancement, and perfection.

Mind, as well as matter, is subject to the same change. Every experience, every thought, every deed, changes a person. There is little resemblance between the elderly and their period of childhood and youth.

An eternally fixed, unchangeable being is not known. Such a being may be assumed, but it is a postulate only. It is not within the range of human observation and knowledge. A being not subject to change would be a being outside progress.

There is a teaching which declares that man has a spiritual soul that is eternally pure, eternally unchanged, eternally perfect, and that sinning, suffering, changing man as we see him is an illusion—that, indeed, the spiritual soul is the man, and the other is unreality.

There is another teaching that affirms that man is eternally imperfect, that stainless purity can never be reached, and that perfection is an impossibility, an illusion.

It will be found that these two extremes have no relation to human experience. They are both of the nature of speculative metaphysics which stand in opposition to the facts of life; so much so that the adherents of these two extremes deny the existence of the commonest everyday facts of human experience. That which is assumed is regarded as real; the facts of life are declared to be unreal.

It is well to avoid both these extremes, and find the middle way of human experience. It is well to avoid opinions and speculations of our own or others, it is well to refer to the facts of life. We see that man passes through birth and growth and old age, that he experiences sin, sickness, and death; that he sorrows and suffers, aspires and rejoices; and that he is ever looking forward to greater purity and striving toward perfection. These are not opinions, speculations, or metaphysics—they are universal facts.

If man were already perfect, there would be no need for him to be perfected, and all moral teaching would be useless and ridiculous. Moreover, a perfect being could not be subject to illusion and unreality.

On the other hand, if a man could never attain to purity and perfection, his aspirations and striving would be useless. They would indeed be mockeries; and the heavenly perfection of saintly and divine men and women would have to be belittled and denied.

We see around us sin, sorrow, and suffering; and we see before us, in the lives of the great teachers, the sinless, sorrowless, divine state. Therefore, we know that man is an imperfect being, yet capable of, and destined for, perfection. The divine state toward which he aspires, he will reach. The fact that he so ardently desires it means that he can reach it, even if the fact were not demonstrated in those great ones who have already attained.

Man is not a compound of two beings, one real and perfect, the other unreal and imperfect. He is one and real, and his experiences are real. His imperfection is apparent, and his advancement and progress are also apparent.

The realities of life claim men in spite of their metaphysics, and all come under the same law of change and progress. He who affirms the eternal sinlessness and perfection of man, should not, to be logical and consistent, ever speak of sins and faults, of disease and death; yet he refers to these things as matters to be dealt with. Thus in theory he denies the existence of that which he habitually recognizes in practice.

He also who denies the possibility of perfection should not aspire or strive; yet we find him practicing self-denial and striving ceaselessly toward perfection.

Holding to the theoretical does not absolve one from the inevitable. The teacher of the unreality of sickness, old age, and death is at last caught in the toils of disease, succumbs to age, and disappears in death.

Change is not only inevitable; it is the constant and unvarying law. Without it, everything would remain forever as it is, and there would be neither growth nor progress.

The strenuous struggle of all life is a prophecy of its perfection. The looking upward of all beings is evidence of their ceaseless ascension. Aspirations, ideals, moral aims, while they denote mans imperfection, assuredly point to his future perfection. They are neither unnecessary nor aimless, but are woven into the fabric of things. They belong to the vital essence of the universe.

Whatsoever a man believes or disbelieves, what theories he holds or does not hold, one thing is certain—he is found in the stream of life, and must think and act. To think and act is to experience; and to experience is to change and develop.

That man is conscious of sin means that he can become pure; that he abhors evil signifies that he can reach up to Good; that he is a pilgrim in the land of error assures us, without doubt, that he will at last come to the beautiful city of Truth.

13

TRANSCENDING DIFFICULTIES AND PERPLEXITIES

"Man who man would be Must rule the empire of himself;
in it Must be supreme, establishing his throne
On vanquished will, quelling the anarchy
Of hopes and fears, being himself alone."

—Shelley

"Have you missed in your aim?
Well, the mark is still shining.
Did you faint in the race?
Well, take breath for the next."

—Ella Wheeler Wilcox

To suggest that any degree of blessedness may be extracted from difficulties and perplexities will doubtless appear absurd to many; but truth is ever paradoxical, and the curses of the foolish are the blessings of the wise. Difficulties arise in ignorance and weakness, and they call for the attainment of knowledge and the acquisition of the strength.

As understanding is acquired by right living, difficulties become fewer, and perplexities gradually fade away, like the perishable mists which they are.

Your difficulty is not contained, primarily, in the situation which gave rise to it, but in the mental state with which you regard that situation and which you bring to bear upon it. That which is difficult to a child presents no difficulty to the matured mind of the man; and that which to the mind of an unintelligent man is surrounded with perplexity would afford no ground for perplexity to an intelligent man.

To the untutored and undeveloped mind of the child how great, and apparently insurmountable, appear the difficulties which are involved in the learning of some simple lesson. How many anxious and laborious hours and days, or even months, its solution costs; and, frequently, how many tears are shed in hopeless contemplation of the unmastered, and apparently insurmountable, wall of difficulty! Yet the difficulty is in the ignorance of the child only, and its conquest and solution is absolutely necessary for the development of intelligence and for the ultimate welfare, happiness, and usefulness of the child.

Even so is it with the difficulties of life with which older children are confronted, and which it is imperative, for their own growth and development, that they should solve and surmount; and each difficulty solved means so much more experience gained, so much more insight and wisdom acquired; it means a valuable lesson learned, with the added gladness and freedom of a task successfully accomplished.

What is the real nature of a difficulty? Is it not a situation which is not fully grasped and understood in all it bearings? As such, it calls for the development and exercise of a deeper insight and broader intelligence than has hitherto been exercised. It is an urgent necessity calling forth unused energy, and demanding the expression and employment of latent power and hidden resources.

It is, therefore, a good angel, albeit disguised; a friend, a teacher; and, when calmly listened to and rightly understood, leads to larger blessedness and higher wisdom.

Without difficulties there could be no progress, no unfoldment, no evolution; universal stagnation would prevail, and humanity would perish of ennui. Let a man rejoice when he is confronted with obstacles, for it means that he has reached the end of some particular line of indifference or folly, and is now called upon to summon up all his energy and intelligence in order to extricate himself, and to find a better way; that the powers within him are crying out for greater freedom, for enlarged exercise and scope.

No situation can be difficult of itself; it is the lack of insight into its intricaçies, and the want of wisdom in dealing with it, which give rise to the difficulty. Immeasurable, therefore, is the gain of a difficulty transcended.

Difficulties do not spring into existence arbitrarily and accidentally; they have their causes, and are called forth by the law of evolution itself, by the growing necessities of the man's being. Herein resides their blessedness.

There are ways of conduct which end inevitably in complications and perplexities, and their are ways of conduct which lead, just as inevitably, out of troublesome complexities. Howsoever tightly a man may have bound himself round he can always unbind himself. Into whatsover morasses of trouble and trackless wastes of perplexity he may have ignorantly wandered he can always find his way out again, can always recover the lost highway of uninvolved simplicity which leads, straight and clear, to the sunny city of wise and blessed action. But he will never do this by sitting down and weeping in despair, nor by complaining and worrying and aimlessly wishing he were differently situated. His dilemma calls for alertness, logical thought, and calm calculation. His position requires that he shall strongly command himself; that he shall think and search, and rouse himself to strenuous and unremitting exertion in order to regain himself. Worry and anxiety only serve to heighten the gloom and exaggerate the magnitude of the difficulty. If he will but quietly take himself to task, and retrace, in thought, the more or less intricate way by which he has come to his present position, he will soon perceive where he made mistakes; will discover those places where he took a false turn, and where a little more thoughtfulness, judgement, economy, or self-denial would have saved him. He will see how, step by step, he has involved himself, and how a riper judgement and clearer wisdom would have enabled him to take an altogether different and truer course. Having proceeded thus far, and extracted from his past conduct this priceless grain of golden wisdom, his difficulty will already have assumed less impregnable proportions, and he will then be able to bring to bear upon it the searchlight of dispassionate thought, to thoroughly anatomize it, to comprehend it in all its details, and to perceive the relation which those details bear to the motive source of action and conduct within himself. This being done, the difficulty will have ceased, for the straight way out of it will plainly appear, and the man will thus have learned, for all time, his lesson; will have gained an item of wisdom and a measure of blessedness of which he can never again be deprived.

Just as there are ways of ignorance, selfishness, folly, and blindness which end in confusion and perplexity, so there are ways of knowledge, self-denial, wisdom, and insight which lead to pleasant and peaceful consummations. He who knows this will meet difficulties in a courageous spirit, and, in overcoming them, will evolve truth out of error, bliss out of pain, and peace out of perturbation.

No man can be confronted with a difficulty which he has not the strength to meet and subdue. Worry is not merely useless, it is folly, for it defeats that power and intelligence which is otherwise equal to the task. Every difficulty can be overcome if rightly dealt with; anxiety is, therefore, unnecessary. The task which cannot be overcome ceases to be a difficulty, and becomes an *impossibility*; and anxiety is still unnecessary, for there is only one way of dealing with an impossibility—namely, to submit to it. The inevitable is the best.

> "Heartily know,
> When half-gods go,
> The gods arrive."

And just as domestic, social, and economic difficulties are born of ignorance and lead to riper knowledge, so every religious doubt, every mental-perplexity, every heart-beclouding shadow, presages greater spiritual gain, is prophetic of a brighter dawn of intelligence for him on whom it falls.

It is a great day in the life of a man (though at the time he knows it not) when bewildering perplexities concerning the mystery of life take possession of his mind, for it signifies that his era of dead indifference, of animal sloth, of mere vegetative happiness, has come to an end, and that henceforth he is to live as an aspiring, self-evolving being. No longer a mere human animal, he will now begin to live as a man, exerting all his mental energies to the solution of life's problems, to the answering of those haunting perplexities which are the sentinels of truth, and which stand at the gate and threshold of the Temple of Wisdom.

> "He it is who, when great trials come,
> Nor seeks nor shuns them, but doth calmly stay."

Nor will he ever rest again in selfish ease and listless ignorance; nor sleekly sate himself upon the swine's husks of fleshly pleasures; nor find a hiding-place from the ceaseless whisperings of his heart's dark and indefinable interrogatories. The divine within him has awakened; a sleeping god is shaking off the incoherent visions of the night, never again to slumber, never again to rest until his eyes rest upon the full, broad day of Truth.

It is impossible for such a man to hush, for any length of time, the call to higher purposes and achievements which is aroused within him, for the awakened faculties of his being will ceaselessly urge him on to the unravelling of his perplexities; for him there is no more peace in sin, no more rest in error, no final refuge but in Wisdom.

Great will be the blessedness of such a man when, conscious of the ignorance of which his doubts and perplexities are born, and acknowledging and understanding that ignorance, not striving to hide himself from it, he earnestly applies himself to its removal, seeks unremittingly, day after day, for that pathway of light which shall enable him to dispel all the dark shadows, dissolve his doubts, and find the solution to all his pressing problems. And as a child is glad when it has mastered a lesson long toiled over, just so a man's heart becomes light and free when he has satisfactorily met some worldly difficulty; even so, but to a far greater degree, is the heart of a man rendered joyous and peaceful when some vital and eternal question which has been long brooded over and grappled with is at last completely answered, and its darkness is for ever dispelled.

Do not regard your difficulties and perplexities as portentous of ill; by so doing you will make them ill; but regard them as prophetic of good, which, indeed, they are. Do not persuade yourself that you can evade them; you cannot. Do not try to run away from them; this is impossible, for wherever you go they will still be there with you—but meet them calmly and bravely; confront them with all the dispassion and dignity which you can command; weigh up their proportions; analyse them; grasp their details; measure their strength; understand them; attack them, and finally vanquish them. *Thus will you develop strength and intelligence; thus will you enter one of those byways of blessedness which are hidden from the superficial gaze.*

14

THE BELIEF THAT SAVES

It has been said that a man's whole life and character is the outcome of his *belief*, and also that his *belief* has nothing whatever to do with his life. *Both statements are true*. The confusion and contradiction of these two statements are only apparent, and are quickly dispelled when it is remembered that there are *two entirely distinct kinds of beliefs*, namely, Head-belief and Heart-belief.

Head, or intellectual belief, is not fundamental and causative, but it is superficial and consequent, and that it has no power in the moulding of a man's character, the most superficial observer may easily see. Take, for instance, half a dozen men from any creed. They not only hold the same theological belief, but confess the same articles of faith in every particular, and yet their characters are vastly different. One will be just as noble as another is ignoble; one will be mild and gentle, another coarse and irascible; one will be honest, another dishonest; one will indulge certain habits which another will rigidly abjure, and so on, plainly indicating that theological belief is not an influential factor in a man's life.

A man's theological belief is merely his intellectual opinion or view of the universe. God, The Bible, etc., and behind and underneath this head-belief there lies, deeply rooted in his innermost being, the hidden, silent, *secret belief of his heart*, and it is this belief which moulds and makes his whole life. It is this which makes those six men who, whilst holding the same theology, are yet so vastly at variance in their deeds—*they differ in the vital belief of the heart.*

What, then, is this heart-belief?

It is that which a man loves and clings to and fosters in his soul; for he thus loves and clings to and fosters in his heart, because he believes in them, and believing in them and loving them, he practises them; thus is his life the effect of his belief, but it has no relation to the particular creed which comprises his intellectual belief. One man clings to impure and immoral things because he believes in them; another does not cling to them because he has ceased to believe in them. A man cannot cling to anything unless he believes in it; belief always precedes action, therefore a man's deeds and life are the fruits of his belief.

The Priest and the Levite who passed by the injured and helpless man, held, no doubt, very strongly to the theological doctrines of their fathers- that was their intellectual belief,- but in their hearts they did not believe in mercy, and so lived and acted accordingly. The good Samaritan may or may not have had any theological beliefs nor was it necessary that he should have; but in his heart he believed in mercy, and acted accordingly.

Strictly speaking, there are only two beliefs which vitally affect the life, and they are, *belief in good* and *belief in evil.*

He who believes in all those things that are good, will love them, and live in them; he who believes in those things that are impure and selfish, will love them, and cling to them. The tree is known by its fruits.

A man's beliefs about God, Jesus, and the Bible are one thing; his life, as bound up in his actions, is another; therefore a man's theological belief is of no consequence; but the thoughts which he harbours, his attitude of mind towards others, and his actions, these, and these only, determine and demonstrate whether the belief of a man's heart is fixed in the false or true.

15

EIGHT PILLARS

Prosperity rests upon a moral foundation. It is popularly supposed to rest upon an immoral foundation—that is, upon trickery, sharp practice, deception and greed. One commonly hears even an otherwise intelligent man declare that "No man can be successful in business unless he is dishonest," thus regarding business prosperity—a good thing—as the effect of dishonesty—a bad thing. Such a statement is superficial and thoughtless, and reveals a total lack of knowledge of moral causation, as well as a very limited grasp of the facts of life. It is as though one should sow henbane and reap spinach, or erect a brick house on a quagmire—things impossible in the natural order of causation, and therefore not to be attempted. The spiritual or moral order of causation is not different in principle, but only in nature. The same law obtains in things unseen—in thoughts and deeds—as in things seen—in natural phenomena. Man sees the processes in natural objects, and acts in accordance with them, but not seeing the spiritual processes, he imagines that they do not obtain, and so he does not act in harmony with them.

Yet these spiritual processes are just as simple and just as sure as the natural processes. They are indeed the same *natural* modes manifesting in the world of mind. All the parables and a large number of the sayings of the Great Teachers are designed to illustrate this fact. The natural world is the mental world made visible. The seen is the mirror of the unseen. The upper half of a circle is in no way different from the lower half, but its sphericity is reversed. The material and the mental are not two detached arcs in the universe, they are the two halves of a complete circle. The natural and the spiritual are not at eternal enmity, but in the true order of the universe are eternally at one. It is in the *unnatural*—in the abuse of function and faculty—where division arises, and where main is wrested back, with repeated sufferings, from the perfect circle from which he has tried to depart. Every process in matter is also a process in mind. Every natural law has its spiritual counterpart.

Take any natural object, and you will find its fundamental processes in the mental sphere if you rightly search. Consider, for instance, the germination of a seed and its growth into a plant with the final development of a flower, and back to seed again. This also is a mental process. Thoughts are seeds which, falling in the soil of the mind, germinate and develop until they reach the completed stage, blossoming into deeds good or bad, brilliant or stupid, according to their nature, and ending as seeds of thought to be again sown in other minds. A teacher is a sower of seed, a spiritual agriculturist, while he who teaches himself is the wise farmer of his own mental plot. The growth of a thought is as the growth of a plant. The seed must be sown seasonably, and time is required for its full development into the plant of knowledge and the flower of wisdom.

While writing this, I pause, and turn to look through my study window, and there, a hundred yards away, is a tall tree in the top of which some enterprising rook from a rookery hard by, has, for the first time, built its nest. A strong, north-east wind is blowing, so that the top of the tree is swayed violently to and fro by the onset of the blast; yet there is no danger to that frail thing of sticks and hair, and the mother bird, sitting upon her eggs, has no fear of the storm. Why is this? It is because the bird has instinctively built her nest in harmony with principles which ensure the maximum strength and security. First, a fork is chosen as the foundation for the nest, and not a space between two separate branches, so that, however great may be the swaying of the tree top, the position of the nest is not altered, nor its structure disturbed; then the nest is built on a circular plan so as to offer the greatest resistance to any external pressure, as well as to obtain more perfect compactness within, in accordance with its purpose; and so, however the tempest may rage, the birds rest in comfort and security. This is a very simple and familiar object, and yet, in the strict obedience of its structure to mathematical law, it becomes, to the wise, a parable of enlightenment, teaching them that only by ordering one's deeds in accordance with fixed principles is perfect surety, perfect security, and perfect peace obtained amid the uncertainty of events and the turbulent tempests of life.

A house or a temple built by man is a much more complicated structure than a bird's nest, yet it is erected in accordance with those mathematical principles which are everywhere evidenced in nature. And here is seen how man, in material things, obeys universal principles. He never attempts to put up a building in defiance of geometrical proportions, for he knows that such a building would be unsafe, and that the first storm would, in all probability, level it to the ground, if, indeed, it did not fall about his ears during the process of erection. Man in his material building scrupulously obeys the fixed principles of circle, square and angle, and, aided by rule, plumbline, and compasses, he raises a structure which will resist the fiercest storms, and afford him a secure shelter and safe protection.

All this is very simple, the reader may say. Yes, it is simple because it is true and perfect; so true that it cannot admit the smallest compromise, and so perfect that no man can improve upon it. Man, through long experience, has learned these principles of the material world, and sees the wisdom of obeying them, and I have thus referred to them in order to lead up to a consideration of those fixed principles in the mental or spiritual world which are just as simple, and just as eternally true and perfect, yet are at present so little understood by man that he daily violates them, because ignorant of their nature, and unconscious of the harm he is all the time inflicting upon himself.

In mind as in matter, in thoughts as in things, in deeds as in natural processes, there is a fixed foundation of law which, if consciously or ignorantly ignored leads to disaster, and defeat. It is, indeed, the ignorant violation of this law which is the cause of the world's pain and sorrow. In matter, this law is presented as *mathematical;* in mind, it is perceived as *moral.* But the mathematical and the moral are not separate and opposed; they are but two aspects of a united whole. The fixed principles of mathematics, to which all matter is subject, are the body of which the spirit is ethical; while the eternal principles of morality are mathematical truisms operating in the universe of mind. It is as impossible to live successfully apart from moral principles, as to build successfully while ignoring mathematical principles. Characters, like houses, only stand firmly when built on a foundation of moral law—and they are built up slowly and laboriously, deed by deed, for in the building of character, the bricks are deeds. Business and all human enterprises are not exempt from the eternal order, but can only stand securely by the observance of fixed laws. Prosperity, to be stable and enduring, must rest on a solid foundation of moral principle, and be supported by the adamantine pillars of sterling character and moral worth. In the attempt to run a business in defiance of moral principles, disaster, of one kind or another, is inevitable. The permanently prosperous men in any community are not its tricksters and deceivers, but its reliable and upright men. The Quakers are acknowledged to be the most upright men in the British community, and, although their numbers are small, they are the most prosperous. The Jains in India are similar both in numbers and sterling worth, and they are the most prosperous people in India.

Men speak of "building up a business," and, indeed, a business is as much a building as is a brick house or a stone church, albeit the process of building is a mental one. Prosperity, like a house, is a roof over a man's head, affording him protection and comfort. A roof presupposes a support, and a support necessitates a foundation. The roof of prosperity, then, is supported by the following eight pillars which are cemented in a foundation of moral consistency:-

1. Energy
2. Economy
3. Integrity
4. System
5. Sympathy
6. Sincerity
7. Impartiality
8. Self-reliance

A business built up on the faultless practice of all these principles would be so firm and enduring as to be invincible. Nothing could injure it; nothing could undermine its prosperity, nothing could interrupt its success, or bring it to the ground; but that success would be assured with incessant increase so long as the principles were adhered to. On the other hand, where these principles were all absent, there could be no success of any kind; there could not even be a business at all, for there would be nothing to produce the adherence of one part with another; but there would be that lack of life, that absence of fibre and consistency which animates and gives body and form to anything whatsoever. Picture a man with all these principles absent from his mind, his daily life, and even if your knowledge of these principles is but slight and imperfect, yet you could not think of such a man as doing any successful work. You could picture him as leading the confused life of a shiftless tramp but to imagine him at the head of a business, as the centre of an organisation, or as a responsible and controlling agent in any department of life—this you could not do, because you realise its impossibility. The fact that no one of moderate morality and intelligence can think of such a man as commanding any success, should, to all those who have not yet grasped the import of these principles, and therefore declare that morality is not a factor, but rather a hindrance, in prosperity, be a sound proof to them that their conclusion is totally wrong, for if it was right, then the greater the lack of these moral principles, the greater would be the success.

These eight principles, then, in greater or lesser degree, are the causative factors in all success of whatsoever kind. Underneath all prosperity they are the strong supports, and, howsoever appearances may be against such a conclusion, a measure of them informs and sustains every effort which is crowned with that excellence which men name success.

It is true that comparatively few successful men practice, in their entirety and perfection, all these eight principles, but there are those who do, and they are the leaders, teachers, and guides of men, the supports of human society, and the strong pioneers in the van of human evolution.

But while few achieve that moral perfection which ensures the acme of success, all lesser successes come from the partial observance of these principles which are so powerful in the production of good results that even perfection in any two or three of them alone is sufficient to ensure an ordinary degree of prosperity, and maintain a measure of local influence at least for a time, while the same perfection in two or three with partial excellence in all, or nearly all, the others, will render permanent that limited success and influence which will, necessarily, grow and extend in exact ratio with a more intimate knowledge and practice of those principles which, at present, are only partially incorporated in the character.

The boundary lines of a man's morality mark the limits of his success. So true is this that to know a man's moral status would be to know—to mathematically gauge—his ultimate success or failure. The temple of prosperity only stands in so far as it is supported by its moral pillars; as they are weakened, it becomes insecure; in so far as they are withdrawn, it crumbles away and totters to ruin.

Ultimate failure and defeat are inevitable where moral principles are ignored or defied—inevitable in the nature of things as cause and effect. As a stone thrown upward returns to the earth, so every deed, good or bad, returns upon him that sent it forth. Every unmoral or immoral act frustrates the end at which it aims, and every such succeeding act puts it further and further away as an achieved realisation. On the other hand, every moral act is another solid brick in the temple of prosperity, another round of strength and sculptured beauty in the pillars which support it.

Individuals, families, nations grow and prosper in harmony with their growth in moral strength and knowledge; they fall and fail in accordance with their moral decadence.

Mentally, as physically, only that which has form and solidity can stand and endure. The unmoral is nothingness, and from it nothing can be formed. It is the negation of substance. The immoral is destruction. It is the negation of form. It is a process of spiritual denudation. While it undermines and disintegrates, it leaves the scattered material ready for the wise builder to put it into form again; and the wise builder is *Morality.* The moral is substance, form, and building power in one. Morality always builds up and preserves, for that is its nature, being the opposite of immorality, which always breaks down and destroys. Morality is the master–builder everywhere, whether in individuals or nations.

Morality is invincible, and he who stands upon it to the end, stands upon an impregnable rock, so that his defeat is impossible, his triumph certain. He will be tried, and that to the uttermost, for without fighting there can be no victory, and so only can his moral powers be perfected, and it is in the nature of fixed principles, as of everything finely and perfectly wrought, to have their strength tested and proved. The steel bars which are to perform the strongest and best uses in the world must be subjected to a severe strain by the ironmaster, as a test of their texture and efficiency, before they are sent from his foundry. The brickmaker throws aside the bricks which have given way under the severe heat. So he who is to be greatly and permanently successful will pass through the strain of adverse circumstances and the fire of temptation with his moral nature not merely not undermined, but strengthened and beautified. He will be like a bar of well-wrought steel, fit for the highest use, and the universe will see, as the ironmaster his finely-wrought steel, that the use does not escape him.

Immorality is assailable at every point, and he who tries to stand upon it, sinks into the morass of desolation. Even while his efforts seem to stand, they are crumbling away. The climax of failure is inevitable. While the immoral man is chuckling over his ill-gotten gains, there is already a hole in his pocket through which his gold is falling. While he who begins with morality, yet deserts it for gain in the hour of trial, is like the brick which breaks on the first application of heat; he is not fit for use, and the universe casts him aside, yet not finally, for he is a being, and not a brick; and he can live and learn, can repent and be restored.

Moral force is the life of all success, and the sustaining element in all prosperity; but there are various kinds of success, and it is frequently necessary that a man should fail in one direction that he may reach up to a greater and more far-reaching success. If, for instance, a literary, artistic, or spiritual genius should begin by trying to make money, it may be, and often is, to his advantage and the betterment of his genius that he should fail therein, so that he may achieve that more sublime success wherein lies his real power. Many a millionaire would doubtless be willing to barter his millions for the literary success of a Shakespeare or the spiritual success of a Buddha, and would thereby consider that he had made a good bargain. Exceptional spiritual success is rarely accompanied with riches, yet financial success cannot in any way compare with it in greatness and grandeur. But I am not, in this book, dealing with the success of the saint or spiritual genius but with that success which concerns the welfare, well-being, and happiness of the broadly average man and woman, in a word, with the prosperity which, while being more or less connected with money—being present and temporal—yet is not confined thereto, but extends to and embraces all human activities, and which particularly relates to that harmony of the individual with his circumstances which produces that satisfaction called happiness and that comfort known as prosperity. To the achievement of this end, so desirable to the mass of mankind, let us now see how the eight principles operate, how the roof of prosperity is raised and made secure upon the pillars by which it is supported.

16

EQUAL-MINDEDNESS

To be equally-minded is to be peacefully-minded, for a man cannot be said to have arrived at peace who allows his mind to be disturbed and thrown off the balance by occurrences.

The man of wisdom is dispassionate, and meets all things with the calmness of a mind in repose and free from prejudice. He is not a partisan, having put away passion, and he is always at peace with himself and the world, not taking sides nor defending himself, but sympathising with all.

The partisan is so convinced that his own opinion and his own side is right, and all that goes contrary to them is wrong, that he cannot think there is any good in the other opinion and the other side. He lives in a continual fever of attack and defence, and has no knowledge of the quiet peace of an equal mind.

The equal-minded man watches himself in order to check and overcome even the appearance of passion and prejudice in his mind, and by so doing he develops sympathy for others, and comes to understand their position and particular state of mind; and as he comes to understand others, he perceives the folly of condemning them and opposing himself to them. Thus there grows up in his heart a divine charity which cannot be limited, but which is extended to all things that live and strive and suffer.

When a man is under the sway of passion and prejudice he is spiritually blind. Seeing nothing but good in his own side, and nothing but evil in the other, he cannot see anything as it really is, not even his own side; and not understanding himself, he cannot understand the hearts of others, and thinks it is right that he should condemn them. Thus there grows up in his heart a dark hatred for those who refuse to see with him and who condemn him in return, he becomes separated from his fellow-men, and confines himself to a narrow torture chamber of his own making.

Sweet and peaceful are the days of the equal-minded man, fruitful in good, and rich in manifold blessings. Guided by wisdom, he avoids those pathways which lead down to hatred and sorrow and pain, and takes those which lead up to love and peace and bliss. The occurrences of life do not trouble him, nor does he grieve over those things which are regarded by mankind as grievous, but which must befall all men in the ordinary course of nature. He is neither elated by success nor cast down by failure. He sees the events of his life arrayed in their proper proportions, and can find no room for selfish wishes or vain regrets, for vain anticipations and childish disappointments.

And how is this equal-mindedness—this blessed state of mind and life—acquired? Only by overcoming one's self, only by purifying one's own heart, for the purification of the heart leads to unbiased comprehension, unbiased comprehension leads to equal-mindedness, and equal-mindedness leads to peace. The impure man is swept helplessly away on the waves of passion; the pure man guides himself into the harbour of rest. The fool says, "I have an opinion;" the wise man goes about his business.

17

ASPIRATION

With the clear perception of one's own ignorance comes the desire for enlightenment, and thus in the heart is born Aspiration, the rapture of the saints.

On the wings of aspiration man rises from earth to heaven, from ignorance to knowledge, from the under darkness to the upper light. Without it he remains a groveling animal, earthly, sensual, unenlightened, and uninspired.

Aspiration is the longing for heavenly things—for righteousness, compassion, purity, love—as distinguished from desire, which is the longing for earthly things—for selfish possessions, personal dominance, low pleasures, and sensual gratifications.

As a bird deprived of its wings cannot soar, so a man without aspiration cannot rise above his surroundings and become master of his animal inclinations. He is the slave of passions, is subject to others, and is carried hither and thither by the changing current of events.

For one to begin to aspire means that he is dissatisfied with his low status, and is aiming at a higher condition. It is a sure sign that he is aroused out of his lethargic sleep of animality, and has become conscious of nobler attainments and a fuller life.

Aspiration makes all things possible. It opens the way to advancement. Even the highest state of perfection conceivable it brings near and makes real and possible; for that which can be conceived can be achieved.

Aspiration is the twin angel to inspiration. It unlocks the gates of joy. Singing accompanies soaring. Music, poetry, prophecy, and all high and holy instruments are at last placed in the hands of those whose aspirations flag not, whose spirit does not fail.

So long as animal conditions taste sweet to a man, he cannot aspire; he is already satisfied. But when their sweetness turns to bitterness, then in his sorrow he thinks of nobler things. When he is deprived of earthly joy, he aspires to the joy which is heavenly. It is when impurity turns to suffering that purity is sought. Truly aspiration rises, phoenix-like, from the dead ashes of repentance, but on its powerful pinions man can reach the heaven of heavens.

The man of aspiration has entered the way which ends in peace, and surely he will reach that end if he neither stays nor turns back. If he constantly renews his mind with glimpses of the heavenly vision, he will reach the heavenly state.

Man attains in the measure that he aspires. His longing to be is the gauge of what he can be. To fix the mind is to foreordain the achievement. As man can experience and know all low things, so he can experience and know all high things. As he has become human, so can he become divine. The turning of the mind in high and divine directions is the sole and needful task.

What is impurity but the impure thoughts of the thinker? What is purity but the pure thoughts of the thinker? One man does not do the thinking of another. Each man is pure or impure of himself alone.

If a man thinks, "It is through others, or circumstances, or heredity that I am impure," how can he hope to overcome his errors? Such a thought will check all holy aspirations and bind him to the slavery of passion.

When a man fully perceives that his errors and impurities are his own, that they are generated and fostered by himself, that he alone is responsible for them, then he will aspire to overcome them. The way of attainment will be opened up to him, and he will see from where and to what destination he is traveling.

The man of passion sees no straight path before him, and behind him is all fog and gloom. He seizes the pleasure of the moment and does not strive for understanding or think of wisdom. His way is confused, turbulent, and troubled, and his heart is far from peace.

The man of aspiration sees before him the pathway up the heavenly heights, and behind him are the circuitous routes of passion up which he has hitherto blindly groped. Striving for understanding, and his mind set on wisdom, his way is clear, and his heart already experiences a foretaste of the final peace.

Men of passion strive mightily to achieve little things—things which speedily perish, and, in the place where they were, leave nothing to be remembered.

Men of aspiration strive with equal might to achieve great things—things of virtue, of knowledge, of wisdom, which do not perish, but stand as monuments of inspiration for the uplifting of humankind.

As the merchant achieves worldly success by persistent exertion, so the saint achieves spiritual success by aspiration and endeavor. One becomes a merchant, the other a saint, by the particular direction in which his mental energy is guided.

When the rapture of aspiration touches the mind, it at once refines it, and the dross of its impurities begins to fall away. While aspiration holds the mind, no impurity can enter it, for the impure and the pure cannot at the same moment occupy the thought. But the effort of aspiration is at first spasmatic and short-lived. The mind falls back into its habitual error, and must be constantly renewed.

The lover of the pure life renews his mind daily with the

invigorating glow of aspiration. He rises early, and fortifies his mind with strong thoughts and strenuous endeavor. He knows that the mind is of such a nature that it cannot remain for a moment unoccupied, and that if it is not held and guided by high thoughts and pure aspirations, it will assuredly he enslaved and misguided by low thoughts and base desires.

Aspiration can be fed, fostered, and strengthened by daily habit, just as is desire. It can be sought, and admitted into the mind as a divine guide, or it can be neglected and shut out. To retire for a short time each day to some quiet spot, preferably in the open air, and there call up the energies of the mind in surging waves of holy rapture, is to prepare the mind for great spiritual victories and destinies of divine import. For such a rapture is the preparation for wisdom and the prelude to peace.

Before the mind can contemplate pure things it must be lifted up to them, it must rise above impure things; and aspiration is the instrument by which this is accomplished. By its aid the mind soars swiftly and surely into heavenly places, and begins to experience divine things. It begins to accumulate wisdom, and to learn to guide itself by an ever-increasing measure of the divine light of pure knowledge.

To thirst for righteousness; to hunger for the pure life; to rise in holy rapture on the wings of angelic aspiration—this is the right road to wisdom. This is the right striving for peace. This is the right beginning of the way divine.

18

RESOLUTION

Resolution is the directing and impelling force in individual progress. Without it no substantial work can be accomplished. Not until a man brings resolution to bear upon his life does he consciously and rapidly develop, for a life without resolution is a life without aims, and a life without aims is a drifting and unstable thing.

Resolution may of course be linked to downward tendencies, but it is more usually the companion of noble aims and lofty ideals, and I am dealing with it in this its highest use and application.

When a man makes a resolution, it means that he is dissatisfied with his condition, and is commencing to take himself in hand with a view to producing a better piece of workmanship out of the mental materials of which his character and life are composed, and in so far as he is true to his resolution he will succeed in accomplishing his purpose.

The vows of the saintly once are holy resolutions directed toward some victory over self, and the beautiful achievements of holy men and the glorious conquests of the Divine Teachers were rendered possible and actual by the pursuit of unswerving resolution.

To arrive at the fixed determination to walk a higher path than heretofore, although it reveals the great difficulties which have to be surmounted, it yet makes possible the treading of that path, and illuminates its dark places with the golden halo of success.

The true resolution is the crisis of long thought, protracted struggle, or fervent but unsatisfied aspiration. It is no light thing, no whimsical impulse or vague desire, but a solemn and irrevocable determination not to rest nor cease from effort until the high purpose which is held in view is fully accomplished.

Half-hearted and premature resolution is no resolution at all, and is shattered at the first difficulty.

A man should be slow to form a resolution. He should searchingly examine his position and take into consideration every circumstance and difficulty connected with his decision, and should be fully prepared to meet them. He should be sure that he completely understands the nature of his resolution, that his mind is finally made up, and that he is without fear and doubt in the matter. With the mind thus prepared, the resolution that is formed will not be departed from, and by the aid of it a man will, in due time, accomplish his strong purpose.

Hasty resolutions are futile.

The mind must be fortified to endure.

Immediately the resolution to walk a higher path is made, temptation and trial begin. Men have found that no sooner have they decided to lead a truer and nobler life than they have been overwhelmed with such a torrent of new temptations and difficulties as make their position almost unendurable, and many men, because of this, relinquish their resolution.

But these temptations and trials are a necessary part of the work of regeneration upon which the man has decided and must be hailed as friends and met with courage if the resolution is to do its work. For what is the real nature of a resolution? Is it not the sudden checking of a particular stream of conduct, and the endeavour to open up an entirely new channel? Think of an engineer who decides to turn the course of a powerfully running stream or river in another direction. He must first cut his new channel, and must take every precaution to avoid failure in the carrying out of his undertaking. But when he comes to the all-important task of directing the stream into its new channel, then the flowing force, which for ages has steadily pursued its accustomed course, becomes refractory, and all the patience and care and skill of the engineer will be required for the successful completion of the work. It is even so with the man who determines to turn his course of conduct in another and higher direction. Having prepared his mind, which is the cutting of a new channel, he then proceeds to the work of redirecting his mental forces—which have hitherto flowed on uninterruptedly—into the new course. Immediately this is attempted, the arrested energy begins to assert itself in the form of powerful temptations and trials hitherto unknown and unencountered. And this is exactly as it should be; it is the law; and the same law that is in the water is in the mind. No man can improve upon the established law of things, but he can learn to understand the law instead of complaining, and wishing things were different. The man who understands all that is involved in the regeneration of his mind will "glory in tribulations," knowing that only by passing through them can he gain strength, obtain purity of heart, and arrive at peace. And as the engineer at last (perhaps after many mistakes and failures) succeeds in getting the stream to flow on peacefully in the broader and better channel, and the turbulence of the water is spent, and all dams can be removed, so the man of resolution at last succeeds in directing his thoughts and acts into the better and nobler way to which he aspires, and temptations and trials give place to steadfast strength and settled peace.

He whose life is not in harmony with his conscience and who is anxious to remedy his mind and conduct in a particular direction, let him first mature his purpose by earnest thought and self-examination, and having arrived at a final conclusion, let him frame his resolution, and having done so let him not swerve from it, let him remain true to his decision under all circumstances, and he cannot fail to achieve his good purpose; for the Great Law ever shields and protects him who, no matter how deep his sins, or how great and many his failures and mistakes, has, deep in his heart, resolved upon the finding of a better way, and every obstacle must at last give way before a matured and unshaken resolution.

19

THE SCIENCE OF SELF-CONTROL

We live in a scientific age. Men of science are numbered by thousands, and they are ceaselessly searching, analyzing, and experimenting with a view to discovery and the increase of knowledge.

The shelves of our libraries, both public and private, are heavy with their load of imposing volumes on scientific subjects, and the wonderful achievements of modern science are always before us—whether in our homes or in our streets, in country or town, on land or sea—there shall we have before us some marvelous device, some recent accomplishment of science, for adding to our comfort, increasing our speed, or saving the labor of our hands.

Yet, with all our vast store of scientific knowledge, and its startling and rapidly increasing results in the world of discovery and invention, there is, in this age, one branch of science which has so far fallen into decay as to have become almost forgotten; a science, nevertheless, which is of greater importance than all the other sciences combined, and without which all science would but subserve the ends of selfishness, and aid in man's destruction—I refer to the *Science of Self-control.*

Our modern scientists study the elements and forces which are outside themselves, with the object of controlling and utilizing them. The ancients studied the elements and forces which were within themselves, with a view to controlling and utilizing them, and the ancients produced such mighty Masters of knowledge in this direction, that to this day they are held in reverence as gods, and the vast religious organizations of the world are based upon their achievements.

Wonderful as are the forces in nature, they are vastly inferior to that combination of intelligent forces which comprise the mind of man, and which dominate and direct the blind mechanical forces of nature. Therefore, it follows that, to understand, control, and direct the inner forces of passion, desire, will, and intellect, is to be in possession of the destinies of men and nations.

As in ordinary science, there are, in this divine science, degrees of attainment; and a man is great in knowledge, great in himself, and great in his influence on the world, in the measure that he is great in self-control.

He who understands and dominates the forces of external nature is the natural scientist; but he who understands and dominates the internal forces of the mind is the divine scientist; and the laws which operate in gaining a knowledge of external appearances, operate also in gaining a knowledge of internal varieties.

A man cannot become an accomplished scientist in a few weeks or months, nay, not even in a few years. But only after many years of painstaking investigation can he speak with authority, and be ranked among the masters of science. Likewise, a man cannot acquire self-control, and become possessed of the wisdom and peace giving knowledge which that self-control confers, but by many years of patient labor; a labor which is all the more arduous because it is silent, and both unrecognized and unappreciated by others; and he who would pursue this science successfully must learn to stand alone, and to toil unrewarded, as far as any outward emolument is concerned.

The natural scientist pursues, in acquiring his particular kind of knowledge, the following five orderly and sequential steps:

1. *Observation*: that is, he closely and persistently observes the facts of nature.
2. *Experiment*: Having become acquainted, by repeated observations, with certain facts, he experiments with those facts, with a view to the discovery of natural laws. He puts his facts through rigid processes of analysis, and so finds out what is useless and what of value; and he rejects the former and retains the latter.
3. *Classification*: Having accumulated and verified a mass of facts by numberless observations and experiments, he commences to classify those facts, to arrange them in orderly groups with the object of discovering some underlying law, some hidden and unifying principle, which governs, regulates, and binds together these facts.
4. *Deduction*: Thus he passes on to the fourth step of deduction. From the facts and results which are before him, he discovers certain invariable modes of action, and thus reveals the hidden laws of things.
5. *Knowledge*: Having proven and established certain laws, it may be said of such a man that he *knows*. He is a scientist, a man of knowledge.

But the attainment of scientific knowledge is not the end, great as it is. Men do not attain knowledge for themselves alone, nor to keep it locked secretly in their hearts, like a beautiful jewel in a dark chest. The end of such knowledge is use, service, the increase of the comfort and happiness of the world. Thus, when a man has become a scientist, he gives the world the benefit of his knowledge, and unselfishly bestows upon mankind the results of all his labors.

Thus, beyond knowledge, there is a further step of *Use*: that is, the right and unselfish use of the knowledge acquired; the application of knowledge to invention for the common weal.

It will be noted that the five steps or processes enumerated follow in orderly succession, and that no man can become a scientist who omits any one of them. Without the first step of systematic observation, for instance, he could not even enter the realm of knowledge of nature's secrets.

At first, the searcher for such knowledge has before him a universe of *things*: these things he does not understand; many of them, indeed, seem to be irreconcilably opposed one to the other, and there is apparent confusion; but by patiently and laboriously pursuing these five processes, he discovers the order, nature, and essences of things; perceives the central law or laws which bind them together in harmonious relationship, and so puts an end to confusion and ignorance.

As with the natural scientist, so with the divine scientist; he must pursue, with the same self-sacrificing diligence, five progressive steps in the attainment of self-knowledge, self-control. These five steps are the same as with the natural scientist, but *the process is reversed*, the mind, instead of being centered upon external things, is turned back upon itself, and the investigations are pursued in the realm of mind (of one's own mind) instead of in that of matter.

At first, the searcher for divine knowledge is confronted with that mass of desires, passions, emotions, ideas, and intellections which he calls himself, which is the basis of all his actions, and from which his life proceeds.

This combination of invisible, yet powerful, forces appears confusedly; some of them stand, apparently, in direct conflict with each other, without any appearance or hope of reconciliation; his mind in its entirety, too, with his life which proceeds from that mind, does not seem to have any equitable relation to many other minds and lives about him, and altogether there is a condition of pain and confusion from which he would fain escape.

Thus, he begins by keenly realizing his state of ignorance, for no one could acquire either natural or divine knowledge, if he were convinced that without study or labor he already possessed it.

With such perception of one's ignorance, there comes the desire for knowledge, and the novice in self-control enters upon the ascending pathway, in which are the following five steps:

1. *Introspection*. This coincides with the *observation* of the natural scientist. The mental eye is turned like a searchlight upon the inner things of the mind, and its subtle and ever varying processes are observed and carefully noted. This stepping aside from selfish gratifications, from the excitements of worldly pleasures and ambitions, in order to observe, with the object of understanding, one's nature, is the beginning of self-control. Hitherto, the man has been blindly and impotently borne along by the impulses of his nature, the mere creature of things and circumstances, but now he puts a check upon his impulses and, instead of being controlled, begins to control.
2. *Self-analysis*. Having observed the tendencies of the mind, they are then closely examined, and are put through a rigid process of analysis. The evil tendencies (those that produce painful effects) are separated from the good tendencies (those that produce peaceful effects); and the various tendencies, with the particular actions they produce, and the definite results which invariably spring from these actions, are gradually grasped by the understanding, which is at last enabled to follow them in their swift and subtle interplay and profound ramifications. It is a process of

testing and proving, and, for the searcher, a period of being tested and proved.

3. *Adjustment.* By this time, the practical student of things divine has clearly before him every tendency and aspect of his nature, down to the profoundest promptings of his mind, and the most subtle motives of his heart. There is not a spot or corner left, which he has not explored and illuminated with the light of self-examination.

   He is familiar with every weak and selfish point, every strong and virtuous quality. It is considered the height of wisdom to be able to see ourselves as others see us, but the practitioner of self-control goes far beyond this: he not only sees himself as others see him, *he sees himself as he is*. Thus, standing face to face with himself, not striving to hide away from any secret fault; no longer defending himself with pleasant flatteries; neither underrating nor overrating himself or his powers, and no more cursed with self-praise or self-pity, he sees the full magnitude of the task which lies before him; sees dearly ahead the heights of self-control, and knows what work he has to do to reach them.

   He is no longer in a state of confusion, but has gained a glimpse of the laws which operate in the world of thought, and he now begins to *adjust* his mind in accordance with those laws. This is a process of *weeding, sifting, cleansing*. As the farmer weeds, cleans, and prepares the ground for his crops, so the student removes the weeds of evil from his mind, cleanses and purifies it preparatory to sowing the seeds of righteous actions which shall produce the harvest of a well ordered life.

4. *Righteousness.* Having adjusted his thoughts and deeds to those minor laws which operate in mental activities in

the production of pain and pleasure, unrest and peace, sorrow and bliss, he now perceives that there is involved in those laws one Great Central Law which, like the law of gravitation in the natural world, is supreme in the world of mind; a law to which all thoughts and deeds are subservient, and by which they are regulated and kept in their proper sphere.

This is the law of Justice or Righteousness, which is universal and supreme. To this law he now conforms. Instead of thinking and acting blindly, as the nature is stimulated and appealed to by outward things, he subordinates his thoughts and deeds to this central principle. He no longer acts from self, *but does what is right*—what is universally and eternally right. He is no longer the abject slave of his nature and circumstances, he is the master of his nature and circumstances.

He is no longer carried hither and thither on the forces of his mind; he controls and guides those forces to the accomplishment of his purposes. Thus, having his nature in control and subjection, not thinking thoughts nor doing deeds which oppose the righteous law, and which, therefore, that law annuls with suffering and defeat, he rises above the dominion of sin and sorrow, ignorance and doubt, and is strong, calm, and peaceful.

5. *Pure Knowledge*. By thinking right and acting right, he proves, by experience, the existence of the divine law on which the mind is framed, and which is the guiding and unifying principle in all human affairs and events, whether individual or national. Thus, by perfecting himself in self-control, he acquires divine knowledge; he reaches the point where it may be said of him, as of the natural scientist, that he *knows*.

He has mastered the science of self-control, and has brought knowledge out of ignorance, order out of confusion. He has acquired that knowledge of self which includes knowledge of all men; that knowledge of one's own life which embraces knowledge of all live—as for all minds are the same in essence (differing only in degree), are framed upon the same law; and the same thoughts and acts, by whatsoever individual they are wrought, will always produce the same results.

But this divine and peace bestowing knowledge, as in the case of the natural scientist, is not gained for one's self alone; for if this were so, the aim of evolution would be frustrated, and it is not in the nature of things to fall short of ripening and accomplishment; and, indeed, he who thought to gain this knowledge solely for his own happiness would most surely fail.

So, beyond the *fifth* step of Pure Knowledge, there is a still further one of *Wisdo*m, which is the right application of the knowledge acquired; the pouring out upon the world, unselfishly and without stint, the result of one's labors, thus accelerating progress and uplifting humanity.

It may be said of men who have not gone back into their own nature to control and purify it, that they cannot clearly distinguish between good and evil, right and wrong. They reach after those things which they think will give them pleasure, and try to avoid those things which they believe will cause them pain.

The source of their actions is self, and they only discover right painfully and in a fragmentary way, by periodically passing through severe sufferings, and lashings of conscience. But he who practices self-control, passing through the five processes, which are five stages of growth, gains that knowledge which enables him to act from the moral law which sustains the universe. He knows good and evil, right and wrong, and, thus knowing them, lives in accordance with good and right. He no longer needs to consider what is pleasant or what is unpleasant, but does what is right; his nature is in harmony with his conscience, and there is no remorse; his mind is in unison with the Great Law, and there is no more suffering and sin; for him evil is ended, and good is all in all.

20

HIDDEN SACRIFICES

"What need hath man
Of Eden passed, or Paradise to come,
When heaven is round us and within ourselves?"

"Lowliness is the base of every virtue:
Who goes the lowest, builds, doubt not, the safest."
—Bailey

"Truth is within ourselves; it takes no rise
From outward things, whate'er you may believe."

—Browning

It is one of the paradoxes of Truth that we gain by giving up; we lose by greedily grasping. Every gain in virtue necessitates some loss in vice; every accession of holiness means some selfish pleasure yielded up; and every forward step on the path of Truth demands the forfeit of some self-assertive error.

He who would be clothed in new garments must first cast away the old, and he who would find the True must sacrifice the false. The gardener digs in the weeds in order that they may feed, with their decay, the plants which are good for food; and the Tree of Wisdom can only flourish on the compost of uprooted follies. Growth—gain—necessitates sacrifice—loss.

The true life, the blessed life, the life that is not tormented with passions and pains, is reached only through sacrifice, not necessarily the sacrifice of outward things, but the sacrifice of the inward errors and defilements, for it is these, and these only, which bring misery into life. It is not the good and true that needs to be sacrificed but the evil and false; therefore all sacrifice is ultimately gain, and there is no essential loss. Yet at first the loss seems great, and the sacrifice is painful, but this is because of the self-delusion and spiritual blindness which always accompany selfishness, and pain must always accompany the cutting away of some selfish portion of one's nature. When the drunkard resolves to sacrifice his lust for strong drink he passes through a period of great suffering, and he feels that he is forfeiting a great pleasure; but when his victory is complete, when the lust is dead, and his mind is calm and sober, then he knows that he has gained incalculably by the giving up of his selfish animal pleasure. What he has lost was evil and false and not worth keeping—nay, its keeping enatiled continual misery—but what he has gained in character, in self-control, in soberness had greater peace of mind, is good and true, and it was necessary that he should acquire it.

So it is with all true sacrifice; it is at first, and until it is completed, painful, and this is why men shrink from it. They cannot see any purpose in abstaining from and overcoming selfish gratification, it seems to them like losing so much that is sweet; seems to them like courting misery, and giving up all happiness and pleasure. And this must be so; for if a man could know that by giving up his particular forms of selfishness his gain in happiness would be immeasurably greater, unselfishness (which is now so difficult of attainment) would then be rendered infinitely more difficult of achievement, for his desire for the greater gain—his selfishness—would thereby be greatly intensified.

No man can become unselfish, and thereby arrive at the highest bliss, until he is willing to lose, looking for neither gain nor reward: it is this state of mind which constitutes unselfishness. A man must be willing to humbly sacrifice his selfish habits and practices because they are untrue and unworthy, and for the happiness of those about him, without expecting any reward or looking for any good to accrue to himself; nay, he must be prepared to lose for himself, to forfeit pleasure and happiness, even life itself, if by so doing he can make the world more beautiful and happy. But does he lose? Does the miser lose when he gives up his lust for gold? Does the thief lose when he abandons stealing? Does the libertine lose when he sacrifices his unworthy pleasures? No man loses by the sacrifice of self, or some portion of self; nevertheless, he thinks he will lose by so doing, and because he so thinks he suffers and this is where the sacrifice comes in—this is where he gains by losing.

All true sacrifice is within; it is spiritual and hidden, and is prompted by deep humility of heart. Nothing but the sacrifice of self can avail, and to this must all men come sooner or later during their spiritual evolution. But in what does this selfabnegation consist? How is it practised? Where is it sought and found? It consists in overcoming the daily proneness to selfish thoughts and acts; it is practised in our common intercourse with others; and it is found in the hour of tumult and temptation.

There are hidden sacrifices of the heart which are infinitely blessed both to him that makes them and those for whom they are made, albeit their making costs much effort and some pain. Men are anxious to do some great thing, to perform some great sacrifice which lies beyond the necessities of their experience, while all the time, perhaps, they are neglecting the one thing needful, are blind to that sacrifice which by its very nearness is rendered imperative. Where lurks your besetting sin? Where lies your weakness? Where does temptation assail you most strongly? There shall you make your first scarifice, and shall find thereby the way unto your peace. Perhaps it is anger or unkindness. Are you prepared to sacrifice the angry impulse and word, the unkind thought and deed? Are you prepared to silently endure abuse, attack, accusation, and unkindness, refusing to pay back these in their own coin? Nay, more, are you prepared to give in return for these dark follies kindness and loving protection? If so, then you are ready to make those hidden scarifices which lead to beatific bliss.

If you are given to anger or unkindness offer it up. These hard, cruel, and wrong conditions of mind never brought you any good; they can never bring you anything but unrest, misery, and spiritual blindness. Nor can they ever bring to others anything but unhappiness. Perhaps you will say: "But he was unkind to me first; he treated me unjustly." Perhaps so, but what a poor excuse is this! What an unmanly and ineffectual refuge! For if his unkindness toward you is so wrong and hurtful yours to him must be equally so. Because another is unkind to you is no justification of your own unkindness, but is rather a call for the exercise of great kindness on your part. Can the pouring in of more water prevent a flood? Neither can unkindness lessen unkindness. Can fire quench fire? Neither can anger overcome anger.

Offer up all unkindness, all anger. "It takes two to make a quarrel;" don't be the "other one." If one is angry or unkind to you try to find out where you have acted wrongly; and, whether you have acted wrongly or not, do nto throw back the angry word or unkind act. Remain silent, self-contained, and kindly disposed; and learn, by continual effort in right-doing, to have compassion upon the wrongdoer.

Perhaps you are habitually impatient and irritable. Know, then, the hidden sacrifice which it is needful that you should make. *Give up your impatience.* Overcome it there where it is wont to assert itself. Resolve that you will yield no longer to its tyrannical sway but will conquer it and cast it out. It is not worth keeping a single hour, nor would it dominate you for another moment if you were not labouring under the delusion that the follies and perversities of others render impatience on your part necessary. Whatever others may do or say, even though they may mock and taunt you, impatience is not only unnecessary, it can never do any other than aggravate the evil which it seeks to remove. Calm, strong, and deliberate action can accomplish much, but impatience and its accompanying irritability are always indiactions of weakness and inefficiency. And what do they bestow upon you? Do they bestow rest, peace, happiness, or bring these to those about you? Do they not, rather, make you and those about you wretched? But though your impatience may hurt others it certainly hurts and wounds and impoverishes yourself most of all.

Nor can the impatient man know aught of true blessedness, for he is a continual source of trouble and unrest to himself. The calm beauty and perpetual sweetness of patience are unknown to him, and peace cannot draw near to soothe and comfort him.

There is no blessedness anywhere until impatience is sacrificed; and its sacrifice means the development of endurance, the practice of forbearance, and the creation of a new and gentler habit of mind. When impatience and irritability are entirely put away, are finally offered up on the altar of unselfishness, then is realised and enjoyed the blessedness of a strong, quiet, and peaceful mind.

"Each hour we think
Of others more than self, that hour we live again,
And every lowly sacrifice we make
For other's good shall make life more than self,
And ope the windows of thy soul to light
From higher spheres. So hail thy lot with lot with joy."

Then there are little selfish indulgences, some of which appear harmless, and are commonly fostered; but no selfish indulgence can be harmless, and men and women do not know what they lose by repeatedly and habitually succumbing to effeminate and selfish gratifications. If the God in man is to rise strong and triumphant, the beast in man must perish. The pandering to the animal nature, even when it appears innocent and seems sweet, leads away from truth and blessedness. Each time you give way to the animal within you, and feed and gratify him, he waxes stronger and more rebellious, and takes firmer possession of your mind, which should be in the keeping of Truth. Not until a man has sacrifice some apparently trivial indulgence does he discover what strength, what joy, what poise of character and holy influence he has all along been losing by that gratification; not until a man sacrifices his hankering for pleasure does he enter into the fulness of abiding joy.

By his personal indulgences a man demeans himself, forfeits self-respect to the extent and frequency of his indulgence, and deprives himself of exemplary influence and the power to accomplish lasting good in his work in the world. He also, by allowing himself to be led by blind desire, increases his mental blindness, and fails of that ultimate clearness of vision, that clarified percipience which pierces to the heart of things and comprehends the real and the true. Animal indulgence is alien to the perception of Truth. By the sacrifice of his indulgences man rises above confusion and doubt, and arrives at the possession of insight and surety.

Sacrifice your cherished and coveted indulgence; fix your mind on something higher, nobler, and more enduring than ephemeral pleasure; live superior to the craving for sense-excitement, and you will live neither vainly nor uncertainly.

Very far-reaching in its effect upon others, and rich with the revelations of Truth for him who makes it, is the sacrifice of self-assertion—the giving up of all interference with the lives, views, or religion of other people, substituting for it an understanding love and sympathy. Self-assertion or opinionativeness is a form of egotism or selfishness most generally found in connection with intellectualism and dialectical skill. It is blindly presumptive and uncharitable, and, more often than not, is regarded as a virtue; but when once the mind has opened to perceive the way of gentleness and self-sacrificing love then the ignorance, deformity, and painful nature of self-assertion become apparent.

The victim of self-assertion, setting up his own opinions as the standard of right and the measure of judgment, regards all those as wrong whose lives and opinions run counter to his own, and, being eager to put others right, is thereby prevented from putting himself right. His attitude of mind brings about him opposition and contradiction from people who are anxious to put him right, and this wounds his vanity and makes him miserable, so that he lives in an almost continual fever of unhappy, resentful and uncharitable thoughts. There can be no peace for such a man, no true knowledge, and no advancement until he sacrifices his desire to bend others to his own way of thinking and acting. Nor can he understand the hearts of others, and enter lovingly into their strivings and aspirations. His mind is cramped and embittered, and he is shut out from all sweet sympathy and spiritual communion.

He who sacrifices the spirit of self-assertion, who in his daily contact with others put aside his prejudices and opinions, and strives both to learn from others and to understand them as they are, who allows to others perfect liberty (such as he exercises himself) to choose their own opinions, their own way in life—such a man will acquire a deeper insight, a broader charity, and a richer bliss than he has hitherto experienced, and will strike a byway of blessedness from which he has formerly shut out.

Then there is the sacrifice of greed and all greedy thoughts. The willingness that others should possess rather than we; the not-coveting of things for ourselves but rejoicing that they are possessed and enjoyed by others, that they bring happiness to others; the ceasing to claim one's "own", and the giving up to others, unselfishly and without malice, that which they exact. This attitude of mind is a source of deep peace and great spiritual strength. It is the sacrifice of *self-interest.* Material possessions are temporary, and in this sense we cannot truly call them our own—they are merely in our keeping for a short time—but spiritual possessions are eternal and must ever remain with us. Unselfishness is a spiritual possession which is only secured by ceasing to covet material possessions and enjoyments, by ceasing to regard things as for our own special and exclusive pleasure, and by our readiness to yield them up for the good of others.

The unselfish man, even though he finds himself involved in riches, stands aloof, in his mind, from the idea of "exclusive possession", and so escapes the bitterness and fear and anxiety which ever accompany the covetous spirit. He does not regard any of his outward accretions as being too valuable to lose, but he regards the virtue of unselfishness as being too valuable to the world—to suffering humanity—to lose or cast away.

And who is the blessed man? He who is ever hankering after more possessions, thinking only of the personal pleasure he can get out of them? or he who is ever ready to give up what he has for the good and happiness of others? By greed happiness is destroyed; by not-greed happiness is restored.

Another hidden sacrifice, one of great spiritual beauty and of powerful efficacy in the healing of human sorrows, is the sacrifice of *hatred*—the giving up of all bitter thoughts against others, of all malice, dislike, and resentment. Bitter thoughts and blessedness cannot dwell together. Hatred is a fierce fire that scorches up, in the heart of him who harbours it, all the sweet flowers of peace and happiness, and makes a hell of every place where it comes.

Hatred has many names and many forms but only one essence—namely, burning thoughts of resentment against others. It is sometimes, by its blind votaries called by the name of religion, causing them to attack, slander, and persecute each other because they will not accept each other's views of life and death, thus filling the earth with miseries and tears.

All resentment, dislike, ill-thinking, and ill-speaking of others is hatred, and where there is hatred there is always unhappiness. No one has conquered hatred while thoughts of resentment towards others spring up in his mind. This sacrifice is not complete until a man can think kindly of those who try to do him wrong. Yet it must be made before true blessedness can be realised and known. Beyond the hard, cruel, steely gates of hatred waits the divine angel of love, ready to reveal herself to him who will subdue and sacrifice his hateful thoughts, and conduct him to his peace.

Whatever others may say of you, whatever they may do to you, *never take offence*. Do not return hatred with hatred. If another hates you perhaps you have, consciously or unconsciously, failed somewhere in your conduct, or there may be some misunderstanding which the exercise of a little gentleness and reason may remove; but, under all circumstances, "Father, forgive them" is infinitely better, sweeter, and nobler than "I will have nothing more to do with them." Hatred is so small and poor, so blind and wretched. Love is so great and rich, so far-seeing and blissful.

> "The highest culture is to speak no ill:
> The best reformer is the man whose eyes
> Are quick to see all beauty and all worth;
> And by his own discreet, well-ordered life
> Alone reproves the erring."

Sacrifice all hatred, slay it upon the holy altar of devotion—devotion to others. Think no more of any injury to your own petty self, but see to it that henceforth you injure and wound no other. Open the flood gates of your heart for the inpouring of that sweet, great, beautiful love which embraces all with strong yet tender thoughts of protection and peace, leaving not one, nay, not even he who hates or despises or slanders you, out in the cold.

Then there is the hidden sacrifice of impure desires, of weak self-pity and degrading self-praise, of vanity and pride, for these are unblest attitudes of mind, deformities of heart. He who makes them, one by one, gradually subduing and overcoming them, will, according to the measure of his success, rise above weakness and suffering and sorrow, and will comprehend and enjoy the perfect and imperishable blessedness.

Now, all these hidden sacrifices which are here mentioned are pure, humble heart-offerings. They are made within; are offered up on the sacred, lonely, unseen altar of one's own heart. Not one of them can be made until the fault is first silently acknowledged and confessed. No man can sacrifice an error until he first of all confess (to himself) "Iam in error;" when, yielding it up, he will perceive and receive the truth which his error formerly obscured.

"The kingdom of heaven cometh not by observation," and the silent sacrifice of self for the good of others, the daily giving up of one's egotistic tendencies, is not seen and rewarded of men, and brings no loud blazon of popularity and praise. It is hidden away from the eyes of all the world, nay, even from the gaze of those who are nearest to you, for no eyes of flesh can perceive its spiritual beauty. But think not that because it is unperceived it is therefore futile. Its blissful radiance is enjoyed by you, and its power for good over others is great and far-reaching, for though they cannot see it, nor, perhaps understand it, yet they are unconsciously influenced by it. They will not know what silent battles you are fighting, what eternal victories over self you are achieving, but, they will *feel* your altered attitude, your new mind, wrought of the fabric of love and loving thoughts, and will share somewhat in its happiness and bliss. They will know nothing of the frequent fierceness of the fight you are waging, of the wounds you receive and the healing balm you apply, of the anguish and the after-peace; but they will know that you have grown sweeter and gentler, stronger and more silently self-reliant, more patient and pure, and that they are rested and helped by your presence. What rewards can compare with this? Beside the fragrant offices of love the praises of men are gross and fulsome, and in the pure flame of a selfless heart the flatteries of the world are turned to ashes. Love is its own reward, its own joy, its own satisfaction; it is the final refuge and resting-place of passion-tortured souls.

The sacrifice of self, and the acquisition of the supreme knowledge and bliss which it confers, is not accomplished by one great and glorious act but by a series of lesser and successive sacrifices in the ordinary life of the world, by a succession of steps in the daily conquest of Truth over selfishness. He who each day accomplishes some victory over himself, who subdues and puts behind him some unkind thought, some impure desire, some tendency to sin, is everyday growing stronger, purer, and wiser, and every dawn finds him nearer to that final glory of Truth which each self-sacrificing act reveals in part.

Look not outside thee nor beyond thee for the light and blessedness of Truth, but look within; thou wilt find it within the narrow sphere of thy duty, even in the humble and hidden sacrifices of thine own heart.

21

PRACTICE OF MEDITATION

When *aspiration* is united to *concentration*, the result is *meditation*. When a man intensely desires to reach and realize a higher, purer, and more radiant life than the merely worldly and pleasure loving life, he engages in *aspiration*; and when he earnestly concentrates his thoughts upon the finding of that life, he practices meditation.

Without intense aspiration, there can be no meditation. Lethargy and indifference are fatal to its practice. The more intense the nature of a man, the more readily will he find meditation, and the more successfully will he practice it. A fiery nature will most rapidly scale the heights of Truth in meditation, when its aspirations have become sufficiently awakened.

Concentration is necessary to worldly success: meditation is necessary to spiritual success. Worldly skill and knowledge are acquired by concentration: spiritual skill and knowledge are acquired by meditation. By concentration a man can scale the highest heights of genius, but he cannot scale the heavenly heights of Truth: to accomplish this, he must meditate.

By concentration a man may acquire the wonderful comprehension and vast power of a Caesar; by meditation he may reach the divine wisdom and perfect peace of a Buddha. The perfection of concentration is power; the perfection of meditation is *wisdom.*

By concentration, men acquire *skill* in the doing of the things of life—in science, art, trade, etc.,—but by meditation, they acquire skill in *life itself*; in right living, enlightenment, wisdom, etc. Saints, sages, saviors—wise men and divine teachers—are the finished products of holy meditation.

The four stages in concentration are brought into play in meditation; the difference between the two powers being one of *direction*, and not of nature. Meditation is therefore *spiritual concentration*; the bringing of the mind to a focus in its search for the divine knowledge, the divine life; the intense dwelling, in thought, on Truth.

Thus a man aspires to know and realize, above all things else, the Truth; he then gives *attention* to conduct, to life, to self-purification: giving attention to these things, he passes into serious *contemplation* of the facts, problems, and mystery of life: thus contemplating, he comes to love Truth so fully and intensely as to become wholly absorbed in it, the mind is drawn away from its wanderings in a multitude of desires, and, solving one by one the problems of life, realizes that profound union with Truth which is the state of abstraction; and thus absorbed in Truth, there is that balance and poise of character, that divine *action in repose*, which is the abiding calm and peace of an emancipated and enlightened mind.

Meditation is more difficult to practice than concentration because it involves a much more severe self-discipline than that which obtains in concentration. A man can practice concentration without purifying his heart and life, whereas the process of purification is inseparable from meditation.

The object of meditation is divine enlightenment, the attainment of Truth, and is therefore interwoven with practical purity and righteousness. Thus while, at first, the time spent in actual meditation is short—perhaps only half an hour in the early morning—the knowledge gained in that half hour of vivid aspiration and concentrated thought is embodied in practice during the whole day.

In meditation, therefore, the entire life of a man is involved; and as he advances in its practice he becomes more and more fitted to perform the duties of life in the circumstances in which he may be placed, for he becomes stronger, holier, calmer, and wiser. The principle of meditation is twofold, namely:

1. Purification of the heart by repetitive thought on pure things.
2. Attainment of divine knowledge by embodying such purity in practical life.

Man is a *thought being*, and his life and character are determined by the thoughts in which he habitually dwells. By practice, association, and habit, thoughts tend to repeat themselves with greater and greater ease and frequency; and so "fix" the character in a given direction by producing that automatic action which is called "habit."

By daily dwelling upon pure thoughts, the man of meditation forms the habit of pure and enlightened thinking which leads to pure and enlightened actions and well performed duties. By the ceaseless repetition of pure thoughts, he at last becomes one with those thoughts, and is a purified being, manifesting his attainment in pure actions, in a serene and wise life.

The majority of men live in a series of conflicting desires, passions, emotions, and speculations, and there are restlessness, uncertainty, and sorrow; but when a man begins to train his mind in meditation, he gradually gains control over this inward conflict by bringing his thoughts to a focus upon a central principle.

In this way the old habits of impure and erroneous thought and action are broken up, and the new habits of pure and enlightened thought and action are formed; the man becomes more and more reconciled to Truth, and there is increasing harmony and insight, a growing perfection and peace.

A powerful and lofty aspiration towards Truth is always accompanied with a keen sense of the sorrow and brevity and mystery of life, and until this condition of mind is reached, meditation is impossible. Merely musing, or whiling away the time in idle dreaming (habits to which the word meditation is frequently applied), are very far removed from meditation, in the lofty spiritual sense which we attach to that condition.

It is easy to mistake reverie for meditation. This is a fatal error which must be avoided by one striving to meditate. The two must not be confounded. Reverie is a loose dreaming into which a man falls; meditation is a strong, purposeful thinking into which a man rises. Reverie is easy and pleasurable; meditation is at first difficult and irksome.

Reverie thrives in indolence and luxury; meditation arises from strenuousness and discipline. Reverie is first alluring, then sensuous, and then sensual. Meditation is first forbidding, then profitable, and then peaceful. Reverie is dangerous; it undermines self-control. Meditation is protective; it establishes self-control.

There are certain signs by which one can know whether he is engaging in reverie or meditation.

The indications of reverie are:

1. A desire to avoid exertion.
2. A desire to experience the pleasures of dreaming.
3. An increasing distaste for one's worldly duties.
4. A desire to shirk one's worldly responsibilities.
5. Fear of consequences.
6. A wish to get money with as little effort as possible.
7. Lack of self-control.

The indications of meditation are:

1. Increase of both physical and mental energy.
2. A strenuous striving after wisdom.
3. A decrease of irksomeness in the performance of duty.
4. A fixed determination to faithfully fulfill all worldly responsibilities.
5. Freedom from fear.
6. Indifference to riches.
7. Possession of self-control.

There are certain times, places, and conditions in and under which it is impossible to meditate, others wherein it is difficult to meditate, and others wherein meditation is rendered more accessible; and these, which should be known and carefully observed, are as follows:

Times, Places, and Conditions in which Meditation is Impossible:

1. At, or immediately after, meals.
2. In places of pleasure.
3. In crowded places.
4. While walking rapidly.
5. While lying in bed in the morning.
6. While smoking.
7. While lying on a couch or bed for physical or mental relaxation.

Times, Places and Conditions in which Meditation is Difficult:

1. At night.
2. In a luxuriously furnished room.
3. While sitting on a soft, yielding seat.
4. While wearing gay clothing.
5. When in company.

6. When the body is weary.
7. If the body is given too much food.

Times, Places, and Conditions in which it is Best to Meditate:

1. Very early in the morning.
2. Immediately before meals.
3. In solitude.
4. In the open air or in a plainly furnished room.
5. While sitting on a hard seat.
6. When the body is strong and vigorous.
7. When the body is modestly and plainly clothed.

It will be seen by the foregoing instructions that ease, luxury, and indulgence (which induce reverie) render meditation difficult, and when strongly pronounced make it impossible; while strenuousness, discipline, and self-denial (which dispel reverie), make meditation comparatively easy. The body, too, should be neither overfed nor starved; neither in rags nor flauntingly clothed. It should not be tired, but should be at its highest point of energy and strength, as the holding of the mind to a concentrated train of subtle and lofty thought requires a high degree of both physical and mental energy.

Aspiration can often best be aroused, and the mind renewed in meditation, by the mental repetition of a lofty precept, a beautiful sentence or a verse of poetry. Indeed, the mind that is ready for meditation will instinctively adopt this practice. Mere mechanical repetition is worthless, and even a hindrance.

The words repeated must be so applicable to one's own condition that they are dwelt upon lovingly and with concentrated devotion. In this way aspiration and concentration harmoniously combine to produce, without undue strain, the state of meditation. All the conditions above stated are of the utmost importance in the early stages of meditation, and should be carefully noted and duly observed by all who are striving to acquire the practice; and those who faithfully follow the instructions, and who strive and persevere, will not fail to gather in, in due season, the harvest of purity, wisdom, bliss, and peace; and will surely eat of the sweet fruits of holy meditation.

22

LIGHT ON THE TRUTH OF TRANSITORINESS

It is well sometimes to meditate deeply and seriously on the truth of Transitoriness. By meditation we will come to perceive how all compounded things must pass away; yea, how even while they remain they are already in the process of passing away. Such meditation will soften the heart, deepen the understanding, and render one more fully conscious of the sacred nature of life.

What is there that does not pass away, among all the things of which a man says, "This will be mine tomorrow"? Even the mind is continually changing. Old characteristics die and pass away, and new ones are formed. In the midst of life all things are dying. Nothing endures; nothing can be retained. Things appear and then disappear; they become, and then they pass away.

The ancient sages declared the visible universe to be Maya, illusion, meaning thereby that impermanency is the antithesis of Reality. Change and decay are in the very nature of visible things, and they are unreal—illusory—in the sense that they pass away forever.

He who would ascend into the realm of Reality, who would penetrate into the world of Truth, must first perceive, with no uncertain vision, the transitory nature of the things of life. He must cease to delude himself into believing that he can retain his hold on his possessions, his body, his pleasures and objects of pleasure. For as the flower fades and as the leaves of the tree fall and wither, so must these things, in their season, pass away forever.

The perception of the Truth of Transitoriness is one of the few great steps in wisdom, for when it is fully grasped, and its lesson has sunk deeply into the heart, the clinging to perishable things which is the cause of all sorrow, will be yielded up, and the search for the Truth which abides will be accelerated.

Anguish is rife because men and women set their hearts on the acquisition of things that perish, because they lust for the possession of those things which even when obtained cannot be retained.

There is no sorrow that would not vanish if the clinging to transient things were given up. There is no grief that would not be dispersed if the desire to have and to hold things which in their very nature cannot endure were taken out of the heart.

Tens of thousands of grief-stricken hearts are today bewailing the loss of some loved object which they called theirs in days that are past, are weeping over that which is gone forever and cannot be restored.

Men are slow to learn the lessons of experience and to acquire wisdom, and unnumbered griefs and pains and sorrows have failed to impress them with the Truth of Transitoriness. He who clings to that which is impermanent cannot escape sorrow, and the intensity of his sorrow will be measured by the strength of his clinging. He who sets his heart on perishable things embraces the companionship of grief and lamentation.

Men and women cannot find wisdom because they will not renounce the clinging to things. They believe that clinging to perishable objects is the source of happiness, and not the cause of sorrow. They cannot escape unrest and enter into the life of peace because desire is difficult to quench, and the immediate and transitory pleasure which gratified desire affords is mistaken for abiding joy.

It is because the true order of things is not understood that grief is universal. It is ignorance of the fleeting nature of things that lies at the root of sorrow.

The sting of anguish will be taken out of life when the lust to hold and to preserve the things of decay is taken out of the heart.

Sorrow is ended for him who sees things as they are; who, realizing the nature of transiency, detaches his heart and mind from the things that perish.

There is a right use for perishable things, and when they are rightly used, and not doted upon for themselves alone, their loss will cause no sorrow.

If a rich man thinks in his heart, "My riches and possessions are no part of me, nor can I call them mine, seeing that when I am summoned to depart from this world, I cannot take them with me; they are entrusted to me to be used rightly, and I mil employ them to the best of my ability for the good of men and for the world," such a man, though surrounded by luxuries and responsibilities, will be lifted above sorrow, and will draw near to the Truth. On the other hand, if the poor man does not covet riches and possessions, his condition will cause him no anxiety and unrest.

He who by a right understanding of life rids his heart of all selfish grasping and clinging, who uses things wisely and in their proper place, and who, with chastened heart, and mind clarified of all thirsty desires, remains serene and self-contained in the midst of all changes, such a man will find Truth. He will stand face to face with Reality.

For in the midst of all error there abides the Truth; at the heart of the transiency there reposes the Permanent; and illusion does but veil the eternal and unchanging Reality.

The nature of that Reality it is not my purpose to deal with here. Let it suffice that I indicate that it is only found by abandoning, in the heart, all that is not of Love and Compassion, Wisdom and Purity. In these things there is no element of transitoriness, no sorrow, and no unrest.

When the truth of Transitoriness is well perceived, and when the lesson contained in the truth of Transitoriness is well learned, then does a man set out to find the abiding Truth; then does he wean his heart from those selfish elements which are productive of sorrow.

He whose treasure is Truth, who fashions his life in accordance with Wisdom, will find the Joy which does not pass away. He will leave behind him the land of lamentation, and, crossing the wide ocean of illusion, will come to the Sorrowless Shore.

23

POVERTY

Many of the greatest men through all ages have abandoned riches and adopted poverty to better enable them to accomplish their lofty purposes. Why, then, is poverty regarded as such a terrible evil? Why is it that this poverty, which these great men regard as a blessing, and adopt as a bride, should be looked upon by the bulk of mankind as a scourge and a plague? The answer is plain. In the one case, the poverty is associated with a nobility of mind which not only takes from it all appearance of evil, but which lifts it up and makes it appear good and beautiful, makes it seem more attractive and more to be desired than riches and honour, so much so that, seeing the dignity and happiness of the noble mendicant, thousands imitate him by adopting his mode of life. In the other case, the poverty of our great cities is associated with everything that is mean and repulsive—with swearing, drunkenness, filth, laziness, dishonesty and crime. What, then, is the primary evil: is it poverty, or is it sin? The answer is inevitable—it is sin. Remove sin from poverty, and its sting is gone; it has ceased to be the gigantic evil that it appeared, and can even be turned to good and noble ends. Confucius held up one of his poor disciples, Yen-hwui by name, as an example of lofty virtue to his richer pupils, yet "although he was so poor that he had to live on rice and water, and had no better shelter than a hovel, he uttered no complaint. Where this poverty would have made other men discontented and miserable, he did not allow his equanimity to be disturbed." Poverty cannot undermine a noble character, but it can set it off to better advantage. The virtues of Yen-hwui shone all the brighter for being set in poverty, like resplendent jewels set in a contrasting background.

It is common with social reforms to regard poverty as the *cause* of the sins with which it is associated; yet the same reformers refer to the immoralities of the rich as being caused by their riches. Where there is a cause its effect will appear and were affluence the cause of immorality, and poverty the cause of degradation, then every rich man would become immoral and every poor man would come to degradation.

An evil-doer will commit evil under any circumstances, whether he be rich or poor, or midway between the two conditions. A right doer will do right howsoever he be placed. Extreme circumstances may help to bring out the evil which is already there awaiting its opportunity, but they cannot cause the evil, cannot create it.

Discontent with one's financial condition is not the same as poverty. Many people regard themselves as poor whose income runs into several hundreds—and in some cases several thousands of pounds a year, combined with light responsibilities. They imagine their affliction to be poverty; their real trouble is covetousness. They imagine their affliction to be poverty; their real trouble is covetousness. They are not made unhappy by poverty, but by the thirst for riches. Poverty is more often in the mind than in the purse. So long as a man thirsts for more money he will regard himself as poor, and in that sense he is poor, for covetousness is poverty of mind. A miser may be a millionaire, but he is as poor as when he was penniless.

On the other hand, the trouble with so many who are living

in indigence and degradation is that they *are* satisfied with their condition. To be living in dirt, disorder, laziness, and swinish self-indulgence, revelling in foul thoughts, foul words and unclean surroundings, and to be satisfied with oneself, is deplorable. Here again, "poverty" resolves itself into a mental condition, and its solution, as a "problem", is to be looked for in the improvement of the individual from within, rather than of his outward condition. Let a man be made clean and alert within, and he will no longer be content with dirt and degradation without. Having put his mind in order, he will then put his house in order; indeed, both he and others will know that he has put himself right by the fact that he has put his immediate surroundings right. His altered heart shows in his altered life.

There are, of course, those who are neither self-deceived nor self-degraded and yet are poor. Many such are satisfied to remain poor. They are contented, industrious, and happy, and desire nothing else; but those among them who are dissatisfied, and are ambitious for better surroundings and greater scope should, and usually do, use their poverty as a spur to the exercise of their talents and energies. By self-improvement and attention to duty, they can rise into the fuller, more responsible life which they desire.

Devotion to duty is, indeed, not only the way out of that poverty which is regarded as restrictive, it is also the royal road to affluence, influence, and lasting joy, yea, even to perfection itself. When understood in its deepest sense it is seen to be related to all that is best and noblest in life. It includes energy, industry, concentrated attention to the business of one's life, singleness of purpose, courage and faithfulness, determination and self-reliance, and that self-abnegation which is the key to all real greatness. A singularly successful man was once asked, "What is the secret of your success?" and he replied, "Getting up at six o' clock in the morning, and minding my own business." Success, honour and influence always come to him who diligently attends to the business of his life, and religiously avoids interfering with the duties of others.

It may here be urged, and is usually so urged, that the majority of those who are in poverty—for instance, the mill and factory workers—have not the time or opportunity to give themselves to any special work. This is a mistake. Time and opportunity are always at hand, are with everybody at all times. Those of the poor above mentioned, who are content to remain where they are, can always be diligent in their factory labour, and sober and happy in their homes; but those of them who feel that they could better fill another sphere, can prepare for it by educating themselves in their spare time. The hard-worked poor are, above all, the people who need to economise their time and energies; and the youth who wishes to rise out of such poverty, must at the outset put aside the foolish and wasteful indulgences of alcohol, tobacco, sexual vice, late hours at music halls, clubs and gaming parties, and must give his evenings to the improvement of his mind in that course of education which is necessary to his advancement. By this method numbers of the most influential men throughout history—some of them among the greatest—have raised themselves from the commonest poverty; a fact which proves that the time of necessity is the hour of opportunity, and not as is so often imagined and declared, the destruction of opportunity; that the deeper the poverty, the greater is the incentive to action in those who are dissatisfied with themselves, and are bent upon achievement.

Poverty is an evil or it is not, according to the character and the condition of mind of the one that is in poverty. Wealth is an evil or not, in the same manner. Tolstoy chafed under his wealthy circumstances. To him they were a great evil. He longed for poverty as the covetous long for wealth. Vice, however, is always an evil, for it both degrades the individual who commits it, and is a menace to society. A logical and profound study of poverty will always bring us back to the individual, and to the human heart. When our social reformers condemn vice as they now condemn the rich; when they are as eager to abolish wrong-living as they now are to abolish low wages, we may look for a diminution in that form of degraded poverty which is one of the dark spots on our civilisation. Before such poverty disappears altogether, the human heart will have undergone, during the process of evolution, a radical change. When that heart is purged from covetousness and selfishness; when drunkenness, impurity, indolence and self-indulgence are driven for ever from the earth, then poverty and riches will be known no more, and every man will perform his duties with a joy so full and deep as is yet (except to the few whose hearts are already pure) unknown to men, and all will eat of the fruit of their labour in sublime self-respect and perfect peace.

24

THE SECRET OF ABOUNDING HAPPINESS

Great is the thirst for happiness, and equally great is the lack of happiness. The majority of the poor long for riches, believing that their possession would bring them supreme and lasting happiness.

Many who are rich, having gratified every desire and whim, suffer from ennui and repletion, and are farther from the possession of happiness even than the very poor.

If we reflect upon this state of things it will ultimately lead us to a knowledge of the all important truth that happiness is not derived from mere outward possessions, nor misery from the lack of them; for if this were so, we should find the poor always miserable, and the rich always happy, whereas the reverse is frequently the case.

Some of the most wretched people whom I have known were those who were surrounded with riches and luxury, whilst some of the brightest and happiest people I have met were possessed of only the barest necessities of life.

Many men who have accumulated riches have confessed that the selfish gratification which followed the acquisition of riches has robbed life of its sweetness, and that they were never so happy as when they were poor.

What, then, is happiness, and how is it to be secured? Is it a figment, a delusion, and is suffering alone perennial? We shall find, after earnest observation and reflection, that all, except those who have entered the way of wisdom, believe that happiness is only to be obtained by the gratification of desire.

It is this belief, rooted in the soil of ignorance, and continually watered by selfish cravings, that is the cause of all the misery in the world.

And I do not limit the word desire to the grosser animal cravings; it extends to the higher psychic realm, where far more powerful, subtle, and insidious cravings hold in bondage the intellectual and refined, depriving them of all that beauty, harmony, and purity of soul whose expression is happiness.

Most people will admit that selfishness is the cause of all the unhappiness in the world, but they fall under the soul-destroying delusion that it is somebody else's selfishness, and not their own.

When you are willing to admit that all your unhappiness is the result of your own selfishness you will not be far from the gates of Paradise; but so long as you are convinced that it is the selfishness of others that is robbing you of joy, so long will you remain a prisoner in your self-created purgatory.

Happiness is that inward state of perfect satisfaction which is joy and peace, and from which all desire is eliminated. The satisfaction which results from gratified desire is brief and illusionary, and is always followed by an increased demand for gratification.

Desire is as insatiable as the ocean, and clamors louder and louder as its demands are attended to.

It claims ever-increasing service from its deluded devotees, until at last they are struck down with physical or mental anguish, and are hurled into the purifying fires of suffering. Desire is the region of hell, and all torments are centered there.

The giving up of desire is the realization of heaven, and all delights await the pilgrim there,

"I sent my soul through the invisible,
Some letter of that after life to spell,
And by-and-by my soul returned to me,
And whispered, I myself am heaven and hell,"

Heaven and hell are inward states. Sink into self and all its gratifications, and you sink into hell; rise above self into that state of consciousness which is the utter denial and forgetfulness of self, and you enter heaven.

Self is blind, without judgment, not possessed of true knowledge, and always leads to suffering. Correct perception, unbiased judgment, and true knowledge belong only to the divine state, and only in so far as you realize this divine consciousness can you know what real happiness is.

So long as you persist in selfishly seeking for your own personal happiness, so long will happiness elude you, and you will be sowing the seeds of wretchedness.

In so far as you succeed in losing yourself in the service of others, in that measure will happiness come to you, and you will reap a harvest of bliss.

It is in loving, not in being loved,
The heart is blessed;
It is in giving, not in seeking gifts,
We find our quest.

Whatever be thy longing or thy need,
That do thou give;
So shall thy soul be fed, and thou indeed
Shalt truly live.

Cling to self, and you cling to sorrow, relinquish self, and you enter into peace. To seek selfishly is not only to lose happiness, but even that which we believe to be the source of happiness.

See how the glutton is continually looking about for a new delicacy wherewith to stimulate his deadened appetite; and how, bloated, burdened, and diseased, scarcely any food at last is eaten with pleasure.

Whereas, he who has mastered his appetite, and not only does not seek, but never thinks of gustatory pleasure, finds delight in the most frugal meal. The angel-form of happiness, which men, looking through the eyes of self, imagine they see in gratified desire, when clasped is always found to be the skeleton of misery. Truly, "He that seeketh his life shall lose it, and he that loseth his life shall find it."

Abiding happiness will come to you when, ceasing to selfishly cling, you are willing to give up. When you are willing to lose, unreservedly, that impermanent thing which is so dear to you, and which, whether you cling to it or not, will one day be snatched from you, then you will find that that which seemed to you like a painful loss, turns out to be a supreme gain.

To give up in order to gain, than this there is no greater delusion, nor no more prolific source of misery; but to be willing to yield up and to suffer loss, this is indeed the Way of Life.

How is it possible to find real happiness by centering ourselves in those things which, by their very nature, must pass away? Abiding and real happiness can only be found by centering ourselves in that which is permanent.

Rise, therefore, above the clinging to and the craving for impermanent things, and you will then enter into a consciousness of the Eternal, and as, rising above self, and by growing more and more into the spirit of purity, self-sacrifice and universal Love, you become centered in that consciousness, you will realize that happiness which has no reaction, and which can never be taken from you.

The heart that has reached utter self-forgetfulness in its love for others has not only become possessed of the highest happiness but has entered into immortality, for it has realized the Divine.

Look back upon your life, and you will find that the moments of supremest happiness were those in which you uttered some word, or performed some act, of compassion or self-denying love. Spiritually, happiness and harmony are, synonymous.

Harmony is one phase of the Great Law whose spiritual expression is love. All selfishness is discord, and to be selfish is to be out of harmony with the Divine order.

As we realize that all-embracing love which is the negation of self, we put ourselves in harmony with the divine music, the universal song, and that ineffable melody which is true happiness becomes our own.

Men and women are rushing hither and thither in the blind search for happiness, and cannot find it; nor ever will until they recognize that happiness is already within them and round about them, filling the universe, and that they, in their selfish searching are shutting themselves out from it.

I followed happiness to make her mine,
Past towering oak and swinging ivy vine.
She fled, I chased, o'er slanting hill and dale,
O'er fields and meadows, in the purpling vale;
Pursuing rapidly o'er dashing stream.
I scaled the dizzy cliffs where eagles scream;
I traversed swiftly every land and sea,
But always happiness eluded me.

Exhausted, fainting, I pursued no more,
But sank to rest upon a barren shore.
One came and asked for food, and one for alms

I placed the bread and gold in bony palms.
One came for sympathy, and one for rest;
I shared with every needy one my best;
When, lo! sweet Happiness, with form divine,
Stood by me, whispering softly, 'I am thine'.

These beautiful lines of Burleigh's express the secret of all abounding happiness. Sacrifice the personal and transient, and you rise at once into the impersonal and permanent.

Give up that narrow cramped self that seeks to render all things subservient to its own petty interests, and you will enter into the company of the angels, into the very heart and essence of universal Love.

Forget yourself entirely in the sorrows of others and in ministering to others, and divine happiness will emancipate you from all sorrow and suffering.

"Taking the first step with a good thought, the second with a good word, and the third with a good deed, I entered Paradise." And you also may enter into Paradise by pursuing the same course. It is not beyond, it is here. It is realized only by the unselfish.

It is known in its fullness only to the pure in heart. If you have not realized this unbounded happiness you may begin to actualize it by ever holding before you the lofty ideal of unselfish love, and aspiring towards it.

Aspiration or prayer is desire turned upward. It is the soul turning toward its Divine source, where alone permanent satisfaction can be found. By aspiration the destructive forces of desire are transmuted into divine and all-preserving energy.

To aspire is to make an effort to shake off the trammels of desire; it is the prodigal made wise by loneliness and suffering, returning to his Father's Mansion.

As you rise above the sordid self; as you break, one after another, the chains that bind you, will you realize the joy of giving, as distinguished from the misery of grasping—giving of your substance; giving of your intellect; giving of the love and light that is growing within you.

You will then understand that it is indeed "more blessed to give than to receive." But the giving must be of the heart without any taint of self, without desire for reward. The gift of pure love is always attended with bliss. If, after you have given, you are wounded because you are not thanked or flattered, or your name put in the paper, know then that your gift was prompted by vanity and not by love, and you were merely giving in order to get; were not really giving, but grasping.

Lose yourself in the welfare of others; forget yourself in all that you do; this is the secret of abounding happiness.

Ever be on the watch to guard against selfishness, and learn faithfully the divine lessons of inward sacrifice; so shall you climb the highest heights of happiness, and shall remain in the neverclouded sunshine of universal joy, clothed in the shining garment of immortality.

Are you searching for the happiness that does not fade away?

Are you looking for the joy that lives, and leaves no grievous day?

Are you panting for the waterbrooks of Love, and Life, and Peace?

Then let all dark desires depart, and selfish seeking cease.

Are you ling'ring in the paths of pain, grief-haunted, stricken sore?

Are you wand'ring in the ways that wound your weary feet the more?

Are you sighing for the Resting-Place where tears and sorrows cease?

Then sacrifice your selfish heart and find the Heart of Peace.

25

BURDEN-DROPPING

"This to me is life;
That if life be a burden, I will join
To make it but the burden of a song."
—Bailey

"Have you heard that it was good to gain the day?
I also say it is good to fall, battles are lost in the same spirit in which they are won."

—Walt Whitman

We hear and read much about burden-bearing, but of the better way of burdendropping very little is heard or known. Yet why should you go about with an oppressive weight at your heart when you might relieve yourself of it and move amongst your fellows heart-free and cheerful? No man carries a load upon his back except to necessarily transfer something from one place to another; he does not saddle his shoulders with a perpetual burden, and then regard himself as a martyr for his pains; and why should you impose upon your mind a useless burden, and then add to its weight the miseries of self-condolence and self-pity? Why not abandon both your load and your misery, and thus add to the gladness of the world by first making yourself glad? No reason can justify, and no logic support, the ceaseless carrying of a grievous load. As in things material a load is only undertaken as a necessary means of transference, and is never a source of sorrow, so in things spiritual a burden should only be taken up as a means towards some good and necessary end, which, when attained, the burden is put aside; and the carrying of such a burden, far from being a source of grief would be a cause for rejoicing.

We say that bodily mortifications which some religious ascetics inflict upon themselves are unnecessary and vain; and are the mental mortifications which so many people inflict upon themselves less unnecessary and vain?

Where is the burden which should cause unhappiness or sorrow? It does not exist. If a thing is to be done let it be done cheerfully, and not with inward groanings and lamentations. It is of the highest wisdom to embrace necessity as a friend and guide. It is of the greatest folly to scowl upon necessity as an enemy, and to wish or try to overcome or avoid her. We meet our own at every turn, and duties only become oppressive loads when we refuse to recognize and embrace them. He who does any necessary thing in a niggardly and complaining spirit, hunting the while after unnecessary pleasures, lashes himself with the scorpions of misery and disappointment, and imposes upon himself a doubly-weighted burden of weariness and unrest under which he incessantly groans.

"Wake thou, O self, to better things;
To yonder heights uplift thy wings;
Take up the psalm of life anew;
Sing of the good, sing of the true;
Sing of full victory o'er wrong;
Make though a richer, sweeter song;

> Out of thy doubting, care and pain
> Weave thou a joyous, glad refrain;
> Out of thy thorns a crown weave thou
> Of rare rejoicing. Sing thou, now."

I will give my cheerful, unselfish, and undivided attention to the doing of all those things which enter into my compact with life, and, though I walk under colossal responsibilities, I shall be unconscious of any troublesome weight or grievous burden.

You say a certain thing (a duty, a companionship, or a social obligation) troubles you, is burdensome, and you resign yourself to oppression with the thought: "I have entered into this, and will go through with it, but it is a heavy and grievous work." But is the thing really burdensome, or is it your selfishness that is oppressing you? I tell you that that very thing which you regard as so imprisoning a restriction is the first gateway to your emanicipation; that work which you regard as a perpetual curse contains for you the actual blessedness which you vainly persuade yourself lies in another and unapproachable direction. All things are mirrors in which you see yourself reflected, and the gloom which you perceive in your work is but a reflection of that mental state which you bring to it. Bring a right, an unselfish, state of heart to the thing, and lo! it is at once transformed, and becomes a means of strength and blessedness, reflecting back that which you have brought to it. If you bring a scowling face to your looking glass will you complain of the glass that it glowers upon you with a deformed visage, or will you put your face right, and so get back from the reflector a more pleasing countenance?

If it is right and necessary that a thing should be done then the doing of it is good, and it can only become burdensome in wishing not to do it. The selfish wish makes the thing appear evil. If it is neither right nor necessary that a thing should be done then the doing of it in order to gain some coveted pleasure is folly, which can only lead to burdensome issues.

The duty which you shirk is your reproving angel; the pleasure which you race after is your flattering enemy. Foolish man! when will you turn round and be wise?

It is the beneficence of the universe that it is everywhere, and at all times, urging its creatures to wisdom as it demands coherence of its atoms. That folly and selfishness entail suffering in ever-increasing degrees of intensity is preservative and good, for agony is the enemy of apathy and the herald of wisdom.

What is painful? What is grievous? What is burdensome? Passion is painful; folly is grievous; selfishness is burdensome.

> "It is the dark idolatry of self
> Which, when our thoughts and actions once are done,
> Demands that man should weep, and bleed, and groan."

Eliminate passion, folly and selfishness from your mind and conduct and you will eliminate suffering from your life. Burden-dropping consists in abandoning the inward selfishness and putting pure love in its place. Go to your task with love in your heart and you will go to it light-hearted and cheerful.

The mind, through ignorance creates its own burdens and inflicts its own punishments. No one is doomed to carry any load. Sorrow is not arbitrarily imposed. These things are self-made. Reason is the rightful monarch of the mind, and anarchy reigns in his spiritual kingdom when his throne is usurped by passion. When love of pleasure is to the fore, heaviness and anguish compose the rear. You are free to choose. Even if you are bound by passion, and feel helpless, you have bound yourself, and are not helpless. Where you have bound you can unbind. You have come to your present state by degrees, and you can recover yourself by degrees, can reinstate reason and dethrone passion. The time to avoid evil is before pleasure is embraced, but, once embraced, its train of consequences should teach you wisdom. The time to decide is before responsibilities are adopted, but, once adopted, all selfish considerations, with their attendant grumblings, whinings, and complainings, should be religiously excluded from the heart. Responsibilities lose their weight when carried lovingly and wisely.

What heavy burden is a man weighted with which is not made heavier and more unendurable by weak thoughts of selfish desires? If your circumstances are "trying" it is because you need them and can evolve the strength to meet them. They are trying because there is some weak spot within you, and they will continue to be trying until that spot is eradicated. Be glad that you have the opportunity of becoming stronger and wiser. No circumstances can be trying to wisdom; nothing can weary love. Stop brooding over your own trying circumstances and contemplate the lives of some of those about you.

Here is a woman with a large family who has to make ends meet on a pound a week. She performs all her domestic duties, down to the washing, finds time to attend on sick neighbours, and manages to keep entirely out of the two common quagmires—debt and despondency. She is cheerful from morning to night, and never complains of her "trying circumstances." She is perennially cheerful because she is unselfish. She is happy in the thought that she is the means of happiness to others. Were she to brood upon the holidays, the pretty baubles, the lazy hours of which she is deprived; of the plays she cannot see, the music she cannot hear, the books she cannot read, the parties she cannot attend, the good she might do, the friendships she is debarred from forming; of the many pleasures which might only be hers if her circumstances were more favourable—if she brooded thus what a miserable creature she would be! How unbearably labourious her work would become! How every little domestic duty would hang like a millstone about her neck, dragging her down to the grave which, unless she altered her state of mind, she would quickly reach, killed by—selfishness! But, not living in vain desires for herself, she is relieved of all burdens, and is happy. Cheerfulness and unselfishness are sworn friends. Love knows no heavy toil.

Here is another woman, with a private income which is more than sufficient, combined with leisure and luxury, yet, because she is called upon to forfeit a portion of her time, pleasure, and money to discharge some obligation which she wishes to be rid of, and which should be to her a work of loving service, or fostering in her heart some ungratified desire, she is perpetually discontented and unhappy, and complains of "trying circumstances". Discontent and Selfishness are inseparable companions. Self-love knows no joyful labour.

Of the two sets of circumstances above depicted (and life is crowded with such contrasted instances) which are the "trying" conditions? Is it not true that neither of them are trying, and that both are blest or unblest in accordance with the measure of love or selfishness which is infused into them? Is not the root of the whole matter in the mind of the individual and not in the circumstance?

When a man, who has recently taken up the study of some branch of theology, religion, or "occultism," says: "If I had not burdened myself with a wife and family I could have done a great work; and had I known years ago what I know now I would never have married." I know that that man has not yet found the commonest and broadest way of wisdom (for there is no greater folly than regret), and that he is incapable of the great work which he is so ambitious to perform. If a man has such deep love for his fellow-men that he is anxious to do a great work for humanity he will manifest that surpassing love always and in the place where he now is. His home will be filled with it, and the beauty and sweetness and peace of his unselfish love will follow wherever he goes, making happy those about him and transmuting all things into good. The love that goes abroad to air itself, and is undiscoverable at home, is not love—it is vanity.

Have I not seen (Oh, pitiful sight!) the cheerless home and neglected children of the misguided missioner and religionist? It is on such self-delusion as this that self-pity and self-martyrdom ever wait, and its self-inflicted misery is regarded by the deluded one as a holy and religious burden which he or she is called upon to bear.

Only a great man can do a great work; and he will be great wherever he is, and will do his noble work under whatsoever conditions he may find himself when he has unfolded and revealed that work.

Thou who art so anxious to work for humanity, to help thy fellow-men, begin that work at home; help thyself, thy neighbour, thy wife, thy child. Do not be deluded; until thou doest, with utmost faithfulness, the nearer and the lesser thou canst not do the farther and greater.

If a man has lived many years of his life in lust and selfish pleasure it is in the order of things that his accumulated errors should at last weigh heavily upon him, as, until they are thus brought home to him, he will not abandon them, will not exert himself to find a better life; but whilst he regards his self-made, self-imposed burdens as "holy crosses" imposed upon him by the Supreme, or as marks of superior virtue, or as loads which Fate, circumstances, or other people have heaped undeservedly and unjustly upon him, he is but lengthening out his folly, increasing the weight of his burdens, and multiplying his pains and sorrows. Only when such a man wakes up to the truth that his burdens are of his own making, that they are the accumulated effects of his own acts, will he cease from unmanly self-pity and find the better way of burden-dropping; only when he opens his eyes to see that his every thought and act is another brick, another stone, built into the temple of his life will he develop the insight which will enable him to recognise his own unstable handiwork, the unflinching manliness to acknowledge it, and the courage to build more nobly and enduringly.

Painful burdens are necessary, but only so long as we lack love and wisdom.

The Temple of Blessedness lies beyond the outer courts of suffering and humiliation and to reach it the pilgrim must pass through the outer courts. For a time he will linger in the outer, but only so long as, through his own imperfect understanding, he mistakes it for the inner. While he pities himself and confounds suffering with holiness he will remain in suffering: but when, casting off the last unholy rag of self-pity, he perceives that suffering is a means and not an end, that it is a state self-originated and self-propagated, then, converted and right-minded, he will rapidly pass through the outer courts, and reach the inner abode of peace.

Suffering does not originate in the perfect but in the imperfect; it does not mark the complete but the incomplete; it can, therefore, be transcended. Its self-born cause can be found, investigated, comprehended, and for ever removed.

It is true therefore, that we must pass through agony to rest, through loneliness to peace; but let the sufferer not forget that it is a "passing through;" that the agony is a gateway and not a habitation; that the loneliness is a pathway and not a destination; and that a little farther on he will come to the painless and blissful repose.

Little by little is a burden accumulated; imperceptibly and by degrees is its weight increased. A thoughtless impulse, a gross self-indulgence, a blind passion yielded to and gratified again and again; an impure thought fostered, a cruel word uttered, a foolish thing done time after time, and at last the gathered weight of many follies becomes oppressive. At first, and for a time, the weight is not felt; but it is being added to day after day, and the time comes when the accumulated burden is felt in all its galling weight, when the bitter fruits of selfishness are gathered, and the heart is troubled with the weariness of life. When this period arrives let the sufferer look to himself; let him search for the blessed way of burden-dropping, finding which he will find wisdom to live better, purity to live sweeter, love to live nobler; will find, in the reversal of that conduct by which his burdens were accumulated, light-hearted nights and days, cheerful action, and unclouded joy.

"Come out of the world—come above it -
Up over its crosses and graves;
Though the green earth is fair and I love it,
We must love it as masters, not slaves,
Come up where the dust never rises -
But only the perfume of flowers -
And your life shall be glad with surprises
Of beautiful hours."

26

WORK, WAGES, AND WELL-BEING

Activity is a necessity of existence, and usefulness is the object of being. Nature at once cuts off that which has become useless. Her economy is faultless, and she will not be burdened with things which have ceased to be of service in her progressive workshop. Nor does she allow her handy tools to lie unused, nor her bright things to rust. Where so ever there is ability, there also are scope and opportunity; where there is energy, there also are legitimate channels for its exercise; where there is a soaring mind, the means of achievement are ready to hand. As the field waits for the plough, the sea for the ship-, and the port for produce, so Nature in all her departments, whether material or mental, stands ready to co-operate with man in all his labors, and to reward him according to his diligence and industry. The statement, "There is no scope for my abilities," is either an expression of vanity, an excuse for negligence, or a confession of lack of resource, or of inability to utilize opportunity. Ability need never lie unused for a moment. There is unlimited scope for all abilities. All that is required is the capacity for work.

Of all abilities, the capacity for work is the most useful and necessary, and its possession is a glorious power; and this men discover when they are disabled, or stricken down with sickness. When they are thus forcibly prevented from engaging in wholesome, invigorating labor, what would they not give to have once again the spirited and glowing use of brain or muscle, or to spend exuberant strength in healthful exertion?

Work is of two kinds- it is either loving labor or enforced slavery. The man whose sole object is to get through his work in order to draw his pay, who has no love for, and no interest in his work, beyond what it represents in cash, is a slave and not a true worker. He labors only under the compulsion of necessity. His entire interest is in getting instead of in doing. He gives his labor irk somely and perfunctorily, but receives his pay with eagerness, striving, when he things he safely can, to give less and less labor, and get more and more wages. "Less work and more pay," is the cry of slaves, and not of men.

On the contrary, the man whose heart is centered in his work, who aims at the perfect performance of his duty, is a true worker whose usefulness and influence are cumulative and progressive, carrying him on from success to greater and greater success, from low spheres of labor to higher and higher still. Thinking little or nothing of the wages, and much of reward, but eager and willing in service, he is sealed by Nature as one of her chosen sons, fitted by virtue of his unselfish labors to receive the greater excellence and fuller reward.

For while full recompense may, and frequently does, escape the man who covetously seeks it, it cannot be withheld from him who ignores it in his work. For the true recompense is never withheld, but in the selfish desire to secure the recompense without giving its equivalent, disappointment is the pay received, and the expected reward does not appear.

The wages of work are sure. In the universal economy no man is cheated; he cannot be defrauded of his just earnings, for every effort receives its proportionate result; first work as the cause, and then wages as the effect. But while wages is the result, it is not the end; it is only a means to a still greater and more far-reaching result and end, namely, the progress and increased happiness both of the individual and the race-in word, to wellbeing.

The receiving of so much money for work done does not represent wages in its entirety; it is, indeed, only a small portion of the actual wages of true work; while the man who considers that the end of work is reached when he has received the money due receives all he bargains for, he does not derive complete satisfaction from his labors, nor comprehend or enter the higher spheres of knowledge and usefulness which are reserved for the devotes of unselfish duty.

It is a day of definitely marked progress in the life of a man when, by the illumination of spirit which proceeds from the development of higher sense of duty, he passes from the burdensome sphere of slavery to the happy world of work; when he leaves behind him the grasping and bartering, the drudgery and humiliation, and, accepting his place among his fellows, becomes a cheerful co-operator with humanity, and a willing and happy instrument in the economy of things.

Such a man receives the completion of wages in its sevenfold fullness as follows:

1. Money
2. Usefulness
3. Excellence
4. Power
5. Independence
6. Honor
7. Happiness

First, he receives the full amount of money of which his work is the equivalent; but in addition to this, his usefulness to the world is increased, and continues to increase in an ever ascending degree; and this greater usefulness is one of the pure delights of labor, for one of the chief rewards of use is to be of greater use. To the slave, idleness is coveted as the reward of labor; but the worker rejoices in more work still.

This accumulating usefulness leads to the wages of excellence-skill, a growing perfection in the work undertaken; and every child that has learned its lesson, and every man and woman that has mastered a problem or a language, or surmounted a great difficulty, is acquainted with the happiness which is the sure accompaniment of such success, although not until later do they realize the full significance of all that is involved in such success in relation to their career.

For a point of excellence is at last reached which merges into power-knowledge, mastery. The man who is devoted to his work becomes at last a master in that work, whatever it may be. He becomes a teacher, a guide, and instructor to others who are treading the lower levels of the path up which he has climbed. He is sought out by others for the knowledge which he has acquired through practice and experience. He is relied upon, and takes his proper place amongst those who lead and serve mankind. Power is a form of wages received as the result of long and arduous labor. It is received only by him who has built it up, so to speak, unselfish toil leads to the reaping of power.

Associated with power is independence. The true worker takes his place among his fellows as a useful citizen. The fearless flash of honesty is in his eyes, the ring of worth is in his voice, and the steadfastness of self-reliance is in his gait. He is not a drone in the human hive, but stands out in shining contrast to the skulking shirker who imagines that the highest good in life is to get something without working for it. The slave who goes to his hated work only because he is whipped to it by necessity comes down to beggary and shame, and is despised and neglected; but the true worker ascends into independence and honor, and is admired and sought.

Honor—This is one of the higher forms of wages, and it comes unerringly and unsought to all who are energetic and faithful in the work of their life. It may be, and often is, late in coming, but come it must and does, and always at its own proper time; for while money is the first and smallest item in wages, honor is one of the last and greatest; and the greater the honor, the longer and harder is the course of labor by which it is earned. There are degrees of honor according to the measure of usefulness, and the greatest men receive the greatest honor.

They who receive the fullness of wages, receive the fullness of happiness, for true work as surely brings about happiness as idleness and enforced labor are paid in the coin of unhappiness. From the perfection of happiness proceeds well-being—a quiet conscience, a satisfied heart, a tranquil mind, and the consciousness of having increased the happiness and aided in the progress of mankind through the full and faithful exercise of one's abilities.

First work, and then wages; but well-being only follows when the work is of the true kind, when it is loved for its own sake, and when the money received for such work is utilized for further work and better achievement instead of being squandered in folly and self-indulgence. Even he who only works for the pay in coin will derive just the measure of well-being which that pay can purchase if he spends it carefully, and will thus aid, in a small measure, industrial progress; but he can also, by a foolish use of his wages, make it an instrument of ill-being, and reduce himself to a dead and useless limb on the tree of life.

It is demanded by the law of things that every man shall receive the equivalent of what he gives. If he gives idleness, he receives inactivity- death; if gives stinted and unwilling service, he receives stinted and hardly secured pay; if he gives loving and generous labor, he recipes generous recompense in a life replete with blessedness.

It may here be asked, "But what about the toiling masses? What you say may be, and doubtless is, true of certain favored individuals, but how can it apply to the vast army of millworks and factory hands, whose toil is long and hard and almost purely mechanical?"

It applies with equal force to them. There are no favored individuals; and there was a time when those who now occupy the high places stood in the low. There is no reason why the mill-worker should not be unselfish in his labor and faithful and conscientious in duty; and there is every reason why he should economize his entire financial, physical, and mental resources, using his money for the improvement of his home and surroundings, and his evenings and spare time in the culture of his intellectual and moral powers. He will thus be preparing himself for higher spheres of usefulness and power, which will not be withheld from him when he is sufficiently equipped and strengthened to deal with intricate matters and carry weighty responsibilities; while the process of preparation itself will be one of ever-increasing knowledge, strength, and happiness.

Work, wages, and well-being are three broad stages in individual and racial evolution; and the political economy of the future will take into account those higher mental and spiritual forms of wages which it now ignores, but which are still the most powerful factors in the well-being of men and nations.

Well indeed will it be for that nation which is the first to realize and wisely utilize the fact that its prosperity and happiness are not limited to its material resources, but that in the mental and spiritual material of its inhabitants it possesses inexhaustible mines of living resources which, when worked with the tools of suitably evolved educational methods, will afford rich yields of prosperity and peace; that the surest and swiftest way to even material success as well as to all the higher and nobler successes is by the assiduous cultivation of character.

27

TRUE HAPPINESS

To maintain an unchangeable sweetness of disposition, to think only thoughts that are pure and gentle, and to be happy under all circumstances,—such blessed conditions and such beauty of character and life should be the aim of all, and particularly so of those who wish to lessen the misery of the world. If anyone has failed to lift *himself* above ungentleness, impurity, and unhappiness, he is greatly deluded if he imagines he can make the world happier by the propagation of any theory or theology. He who is daily living in harshness, impurity, or unhappiness is day by day adding to the sum of the world's misery; whereas he who continually lives in goodwill, and does not depart from happiness, is day by day increasing the sum of the world's happiness, and this independently of any religious beliefs which these may or may not hold.

He who has not learned how to be gentle, or giving, loving and happy, has learned very little, great though his book-learning and profound his acquaintance which the letter of Scripture may be, for it is in the process of *becoming* gentle, pure, and happy that the deep, real and enduring lessons of life are learned. Unbroken sweetness of conduct in the face of all outward antagonism is the infallible indication of a self-conquered soul, the witness of wisdom, and the proof of the possession of Truth.

A sweet and happy soul is the ripened fruit of experience and wisdom, and it sheds abroad the invisible yet powerful aroma of its influence, gladdening the hearts of others, and purifying the world. And all who will, and who have not yet commenced, may begin *this day*, if they will so resolve, to live sweetly and happily, as becomes the dignity of a true manhood or womanhood. Do not say that your surroundings are against you. A man's surroundings are *never* against him; they are there to aid him, and all those outward occurrences over which you lose sweetness and peace of mind are the very conditions necessary to your development, and it is only by meeting and overcoming them that you can learn, and grow, and ripen. The fault is in yourself.

Pure happiness is the rightful and healthy condition of the soul, and all may possess it if they will live purely and unselfish.

> "Have goodwill
> To all that lives, letting unkindness die,
> And greed and wrath, so that your lives be made
> Like soft airs passing by."

Is this too difficult for you? Then unrest and unhappiness will continue to dwell with you. Your belief and aspiration and resolve are all that are necessary to make it easy, to render it in the near future a thing accomplished, a blessed state realised.

Despondency, irritability, anxiety and complaining, condemning and grumbling all these are thought-cankers, mind-diseases; they are the indications of a wrong mental condition, and those who suffer therefrom would do well to remedy their thinking and conduct. It is true there is much sin and misery in the world, so that all our love and compassion are needed, but our misery is not needed- there is already too much of that. No, it is our cheerfulness and happiness that are needed for there is too little of that. We can give nothing better to the world than beauty of life and character;

without this, all other things are vain; this is pre-eminently excellent; it is enduring, real, and not to be overthrown, and it includes all joy and blessedness.

Cease to dwell pessimistically upon the wrongs around you; dwell no more in complaints about, and revolt against, the evil in others, and commence to live free from all wrong and evil yourself. Peace of mind, pure religion, and true reform lie this way. If you would have others true, be true; if you would have the world emancipated from misery and sin, emancipate yourself; if you would have your home and your surroundings happy, be happy. You can transform everything around you if you will transform yourself.

> "Don't bewail and bemoan..
> Don't waste yourself in rejection, nor bark against the bad,
> but chant the beauties of the good."

And this you will naturally and spontaneously do as you realise the good in yourself.

28

THE TEMPLE OF PROSPERITY

The reader who has followed the course of this book with a view to obtaining information on the details of money making, business transactions, profit and loss in various undertakings, prices, markets, agreements, contracts, and other matters connected with the achievement of prosperity, will have noted an entire absence of any instruction on these matters of detail. The reason for this is fourfold, namely:-

First. Details cannot stand alone, but are powerless to build up anything unless intelligently related to principles.

Second. Details are infinite, and are ceaselessly changing, while principles are few, and are eternal and unchangeable.

Third. Principles are the coherent factors in all details, regulating and harmonizing them, so that to have right principles is to be right in all the subsidiary details.

Fourth. A teacher of truth in any direction *must* adhere rigidly to principles, and must not allow himself to be drawn away from them into the ever-changing maze of private particulars and personal details, because such particulars and details have only a local right, and are only necessary for certain individuals, while principles are universally right and are necessary for all men.

He who grasps the principles of this book so as to be able to intelligently practice them, will be able to reach the heart of this fourfold reason. The details of a man's affairs are important, but they are *his* details or the details of his particular branch of industry, and all outside that branch are not concerned with them, but moral principles are the same for all men; they are applicable to all conditions, and govern all particulars.

The man who works from fixed principles does not need to harass himself over the complications of numerous details. He will grasp, as it were, the entire details in one single thought, and will see them through and through, illumined by the light of the principle to which they stand related, and this without friction, and with freedom from anxiety and strain.

Until principles are grasped, details are regarded, and dealt with, as primary matters, and so viewed they lead to innumerable complications and confused issues. In the light of principles, they are seen to be secondary facts, and so seen, all difficulties connected with them are at once overcome and annulled by a reference to principles.

He who is involved in numerous details without the regulating and synthesizing element of principles is like one lost in a forest, with no direct path along which to walk amid the mass of objects. He is swelled up by the details, while the man of principles contains all details within himself; he stands outside them, as it were, and grasps them in their entirety, while the other man can only see the few that are nearest to him at the time.

All things are contained in principles. They are the laws of things, and all things observe their own law. It is an error to view things apart from their nature. Details are the letter of which principles are the spirit. It is as true in art, science, literature, commerce, as in religion, that "the letter killeth, the spirit of giveth life." The body of a man, with its wonderful combination of parts, is important, but only in its relation to the spirit. The spirit being withdrawn, the body is useless and is put away. The body of a business, with all its complicated details is important, but only in its relation to the vivifying principles by which it is controlled. These withdrawn, the business will perish.

To have the body of prosperity—its material presentation—we must first have the spirit of prosperity, and the spirit of prosperity is the quick spirit of moral virtue. Moral blindness prevails. Men see money, property, pleasure, leisure, etc., and, mistaking them for prosperity, strive to get them for their own enjoyment, but, when obtained, they find no enjoyment in them.

Prosperity is at first a spirit, an attitude of mind, a moral power, a life, which manifests outwardly in the form of plenty, happiness, joy. Just as a man cannot become a genius by writing poems, essay as plays, but must develop and acquire the soul of genius—when the writing will follow as effect to cause-so one cannot become prosperous by hoarding up money, and by gaining property and possessions, but must develop and acquire the soul of virtue, when the material accessories will follow as effect to cause, for the spirit of virtue is the spirit of joy, and it contains within itself all abundance, all satisfaction, all fullness of life.

There is no joy in money, there is no joy in property, there is no joy in material accumulations or in any material things of itself. These things are dead and lifeless. The spirit of joy must be in the man or it is nowhere. He must have within him the capacity for happiness. He must have the wisdom to know how to use these things, and not merely hoard them. He must possess them, and not be possessed by them. They must be dependent upon him, and not he upon them. They must be dependent upon him, and not he upon them. They must follow him, and not be for ever be running after them; and they will inevitably follow him, if he has the moral elements within to which they are related.

Nothing is absent from the Kingdom of heaven; it contains all good, true, and necessary things, and "the Kingdom of God is within you." I know rich people who are supremely happy, because they are generous, magnanimous, pure and joyful; but I also know rich people who are very miserable, and these are they who looked to money and possessions for their happiness, and have not developed the spirit of good and of joy within themselves.

How can it be said of a wretched man that he is "prosperous", even if his income be ten thousand pounds a year? There must be fitness, and harmony, and satisfaction in a true prosperity. When a rich man is happy, it is that he brought the spirit of happiness to his riches, and not that the riches brought happiness to him. He is a full man with full material advantages and responsibilities, while the miserable rich man is an empty man looking to riches for that fullness of life which can only be evolved from within.

Thus prosperity resolves itself into a moral capacity, and in the wisdom to rightfully use and lawfully enjoy the material things which are inseparable from our earthly life. If one would be free without, let him first be free within, for if he be bound in a spirit by weakness, selfishness, or vice, how can the possession of money liberate him! Will it not rather become, in his hands, a ready instrument by which to further enslave himself?

The visible effects of prosperity, then, must not be considered alone, but in their relation to the mental and moral cause. There is a hidden foundation to every building; the fact that it continues to stands is proof of that. There is a hidden foundation to every from of established success; its permanence proves that it is so. Prosperity stands on the foundation of *character,* and there is not, in all the wide universe, any other foundation. True wealth is weal, welfare, well being, soundness, wholeness, and happiness. The wretched rich are not truly wealthy. They are merely encumbered with money, luxury, and leisure, as instruments of self torture. By their possessions they are self cursed.

The moral man is ever blessed, ever happy, and his life, viewed as a whole, is always a success. To these there is no exception, for whatever failures he may have in detail, the finished work of his life will be sound, whole, complete; and through all he will have a quiet conscience, an honorable name, and all manifold blessings which are inseparable from richness of character, and without this moral richness, financial riches will not avail or satisfy.

Let us briefly recapitulate, and again view the Eight Pillars in their strength and splendour.

Energy—Rousing one's self up to strenuous and unremitting exertion in the accomplishment of one's task.

Economy—Concentration of power, the conservation of both capital and character, the latter being mental capital, and therefore of the utmost importance.

Integrity—Unswerving honesty; keeping inviolate all promises, agreements, and contracts, apart from all considerations of loss or gain.

System—Making all details, subservient to order, and thereby relieving the memory and the mind of superfluous work and strain by reducing many to one.

Sympathy—Magnanimity, generosity, gentleness, and tenderness; being open handed, free, and kind.

Sincerity—Being sound and whole, robust and true; and therefore not being one person in public and another in private, and not assuming good actions openly while doing bad actions in secret.

Impartiality—Justice; not striving for self, but weighing both sides, and acting in accordance with equity.

Self-Reliance—Looking to one's self only for strength and support by standing on principles which are fixed and invincible, and not relying upon outward things which at any moment may be snatched away.

How can any life be other than successful which is built on these Eight Pillars? Their strength is such that no physical or intellectual strength can compare with it; and to have built all the eight perfectly would render a man invincible. It will be found, however, that men are often strong in one or several of these qualities, and weak in others, and it is this weak element that invites failure. It is foolish, for instance, to attribute a man's failure in business to his honest. It is impossible for honesty to produce failure. The cause of failure must be looked for in some other direction—in the lack, and not the possession, of some good necessary quality. Moreover, such attribution of failure to honesty is a slur on the integrity of commerce; and a false indictment of those men, numerous enough, who are honourably engaged in trade. A man may be strong in Energy, Economy, and System, but comparatively weak in the other five. Such a man will just fail of complete success by lacking one of the four corner pillars, namely, Integrity. His temple will give way at that weak corner, for the first four Pillars *must* be well built before the Temple of Prosperity can stand secure. They are the first qualities to be acquired in a man's moral evolution, and without them the second four cannot be possessed. Again, if a man be strong in the first three, and lack the fourth, the absence of order will invite confusion and disaster into his affairs; and so on with any partial combination of these qualities, especially of the first four, for the second four are of so lofty a character that at present men can but possess them, with rare exceptions, in a more or less imperfect form. The man of the world, then, who wishes to secure an abiding success in any branch of commerce, or in one of the many lines of industry in which men are commonly engaged, *must* build into his character, by practice, the first four moral Pillars. By these fixed principles he must regulate his thought, his conduct, and his affairs; consulting them in every difficulty, making every detail serve them, and above all, *never deserting them under any circumstance to gain some personal advantage or to save some personal trouble,* for to so desert them is to make one's self vulnerable to the disintegrating elements of evil, and to become assailable to accusations from others. He who so abides by these four principles will achieve a full measure of success in his own particular work, whatever it may be; his Temple of Prosperity will be well built and well supported, and it will stand secure. The perfect practice of these four principles is within the scope of all men who are willing to study them with that object in view, for they are so simple and plain that a child could grasp their meaning, and their perfection in conduct does not call for an unusual degree of self sacrifice, though it demands some self denial and personal discipline without which there can be no success in this world of action. The second four pillars, however, are principles of a more profound nature, are more difficult to understand and practice, and call from the highest degree of self sacrifice and self effacement. Few, at present, can reach that detachment from the personal element which their perfect practice demands, but the few who accomplish this in any marked degree will vastly enlarge their powers and enrich their life, and will adorn their Temple of Prosperity with a singular and attractive beauty which will gladden and elevate all beholders long after they have passed away.

But those who are beginning to build their Temple of Prosperity in accordance with the teaching of this book, must bear in mind that a building requires time to erect, and it must be patiently raised up, brick upon brick and stone upon stone, and the Pillars must be firmly fixed and cemented, and labour and care will be needed to make the whole complete. And the building of this inner mental Temple is none the less real and substantial because invisible and noiseless, for in the raising up of his, as of Solomon's Temple which was "seven years in building"—it can be said, "there was neither hammer nor axe nor any tool of iron heard in the house, while it was in the building".

Even so, oh reader construct thy character, raise up the house of thy life, build up thy Temple of Prosperity. Be not as the foolish who rise and fall upon the uncertain flux of selfish desires: but be at peace in thy labour, crown thy career with completeness, and so be numbered among the wise who, without uncertainty, build upon a fixed and secure foundation—even upon the Principles of Truth which endure for ever.